The Dumb Zone
A snarky look at your Obsessive Climbing Disorder
Leah Carson

Published by Excellent Words LLC

ISBN 978-0-9836412-8-5

For information, contact:
Excellent Words LLC
P.O. Box 253
Dousman WI 53118

All photos copyright iStockphoto.com (except author photo, from author's priceless collection).

Book design by Michael Campbell, MC Writing Services

Visit our website at www.carsonmania.com

Substandard Cover-Your-Arse Legalese: Everything the author knows about climbing (and it isn't much) comes from books, documentaries, websites, and lurking around sporting gear stores in Colorado and Utah. Mistaking her for a competent authority won't get you 10 feet off the ground and may incur physical peril, emotional turmoil, and financial ruin.

THE DUMB ZONE

A snarky look at your
***O**bsessive **C**limbing **D**isorder*

LEAH CARSON

DISCOVER YOUR HIGH-Q

Dopey beginner? Gonzo hill climber? Rockhead? Elite hard-guy/gal with a death wish? Let's be brutally honest about your climbing status. You won't get anything out of this book unless you know where you stand.

Actually, you might not get anything out of this book except a few laughs. *Brutally honest* just sounds really badass. And badass is what climbing's all about.

So go ahead. Discover your High-Q.

1. When you hear "Khumbu Icefall," you think…
   a) I dunno—is that, like, Disney on Ice?
   b) an unavoidable section of Mt. Everest that scares the living crap out of me.
   c) that's not my thing, man.
   d) with all those ladders and ropes, my two-year-old daughter could climb there.

2. After a long climbing session, you like to…
   a) go home and play videogames online.
   b) get plastered with buddies around a campfire.
   c) rappel down to the base and start all over again.
   d) hang upside down in a bivy sack battered by an ice storm at 18,000 ft.

3. Getting the green light for your latest climb involved…
   a) sneaking into a McDonald's PlayPlace when nobody was looking.
   b) filling out a park permit listing my next of kin.
   c) outfoxing the park rangers near the hippie encampment.
   d) praying to the mountain gods at Khamingabublamooga Slivovitz Base Camp.

4. While browsing an adventure-outfitter store, you spot a
   $2,700 auto-belay. Your first reaction…
   a) I'm in the wrong store.
   b) I'm in the wrong aisle.
   c) Could I walk out of here with that thing under my tee
      shirt?
   d) My kids can live on peanut butter sandwiches for
      another season.

5. Your typical injury would be a…
   a) blister on my thumb.
   b) dislocated shoulder.
   c) total loss of fingerprints.
   d) broken neck.

6. Your closest friends…
   a) think I'll get tired of going to the climbing gym pretty
      soon.
   b) let me bum a ride to the base in their mom's car.
   c) will climb with me on an hour's notice.
   d) are the two who are still alive.

7. Your spirit animal is a…
   a) panda.
   b) mountain goat.
   c) spider.
   d) 2,400-year-old piece of lichen clinging to a Patago-
      nian ice wall.

8. The only thing that might tempt you to stop climbing
   would be…
   a) just about anything.
   b) some other sport requiring even more gear.
   c) cliff jumping.
   d) death.

9. Growing up, you wanted to be…
   a) a rock star.
   b) a movie stuntman.
   c) a monkey.
   d) God.

10. Ten years from now, you see yourself as…
   a) a couch potato.
   b) earning money from endorsements.
   c) taking time off to heal all 10 of my finger pulley tears.
   d) having my body airlifted out of Nepal.

Scoring

Mostly A's: Turn to Part I: Wannabes and Newbies. Take all the time you need. It could be years.

Mostly B's: Ever heard the saying "You don't know what you don't know"? Read Part II: Freaks and Geeks, because what *you* don't know could kill you.

Mostly C's: All in all, you're just another fly on the wall. Check out Part III½: Rockheads.

Mostly D's: You won't be surprised by Part III: Hardcores, because you already know it's loony at the top.

FALL
Climbing's Four-letter F-word

Shouldn't say it.
Shouldn't think it.

Now you can't get it out of your mind.

Fall Fall Fall Fall Fall

FallFallFallFallFallFallFall

"Aaaaaiiiiiyyyyyeeeee!"

To Tom,

who cheerfully endures my obsessive writing disorder

X

TABLE OF NONSENSE

PART I
GROUND LEVEL:
WANNABES AND NEWBIES

Habitat: gym climbing wall, neighbor's garden shed, puny rock
next to trailhead parking lot

Skill level: ranges from None to Ridiculously Lame

So you wanna be a climber, huh? Bowling's not good enough for you? Ice fishing was boring? The Coast Guard had to rescue you in that rented kayak?

Somehow you caught the climbing bug. Maybe while watching one of the 500+ IMAX films about Everest. Or vacationing in a mountain village where elite climbers occupy the top of the food chain. You might have seen a free-climber scampering over a sheer rock face and thought, *I can do that.*

I've gotta break it to you, pudding head: it's way harder than you think. To begin your climbing career, you've got to crawl up the wall. Not a rock wall, either. Not even a boulder. Just a dinky little wall in the not-so-great indoors: the gym climbing wall.

CALLING ALL GYM RATS

~~~~~~~~~~~~~~~~~~

At first glance, a climbing wall looks like the underside of a school-boy's desk littered with ABC gum (Already Been Chewed). While those handholds might seem randomly placed, they're arranged to set you up for a fall.

No, the staff doesn't hope you plunge to your death—after all, the liability would cut into their profits. But they do need to make your climbs increasingly harder so you keep renewing your gym membership. Eventually you'll be ready for the real thing outdoors.

For you, for now, that pimply wall is as easy as it gets. If you can't make it there, you can't make it anywhere. And you can't blame your lousy performance on weather or variable rock conditions. Worn-out polyurethane, maybe. But nobody will believe you.

"Holds" that thought

The holds have strange names like crack, sloper, sag, grip loss, carpal tunnel, arthritis and tendinitis.

They're like the natural holds on boulders or rock faces, except Mother Nature doesn't make the easy ones bright pink and the harder ones navy blue.

Using the holds teaches you various hand positions: cling, under-cling, overcling, clutch, panic paralysis, and crap out. Before long you'll understand why they sound increasingly desperate.

Don't you just hate being outclimbed by a 5-year-old?

Tears for fears

Mental blocks create big problems for gym-wall climbers. Most common are fear of failing, fear of falling, and fear of being stuck near the ceiling at closing time when they turn off all the lights. These are understandable, but don't let them stop you—unless you make a habit of failing, falling, and getting stranded after hours.

In that case you should listen to your amygdala, the primitive part of your brain that shouts "Knock it off, dummy!" Ask the gym for a refund, or try a piece of equipment that sits closer to the ground, like a recumbent stationary bike.

But let's say you somehow inched your way up the steepest gym wall. That doesn't mean you're a climber. More of a creeper, like a bedbug.

Let's take a second look at some important gym-climbing facts I haven't mentioned.

Δ When most climbers have mastered a given route, the instructors rearrange the holds overnight without telling anyone.

Δ At some gyms you can rent climbing shoes. The previous renter probably didn't wear socks and might've had trench foot, athlete's foot or something-other foot. Bring socks.

Δ Women with stylish 10-inch lacquered fingernails should avoid climbing and take up the 100-meter dash instead.

Δ Guys: don't sneak up behind a woman on the wall with a suave opener like "Hey, babe, you climb here often?" She just might fart in your face.

A screw-it-yourself home climbing wall

Home climbing walls are becoming more popular all the time. If you have acrophobia (fear of heights), agoraphobia (fear of leaving home) or fartophobia (fear of getting farted in the face), this might be your best option. Shut out the real world and just climb your wimpy wall over and over and over-and-out.

Building the wall will be a blast if you're a master carpenter. If not, sketch your dream wall on a cocktail napkin and hire somebody who knows their way around a circular saw. Then take a tip from the Tommy Caldwell Home Safety Manual: steer clear of their workshop and keep your climbing appendages intact.

As for the home wall's location, consider how the space is used. *Garage:* Will Dad's SUV fit underneath the wall? What if you fall through his moon roof? *The kitchen:* Definitely avoid climbing above a hot cooking surface or a knife rack. *The back yard:* What's in your fall zone: a moldy swimming pool? a bed of thistles? the neighbors' bloodthirsty Doberman?

Keep at it, whether you're climbing at the gym or on your home wall. Keep climbing, falling, getting back up and climbing some more until your hands reek of polyurethane and you see bright plastic blobs in your dreams.

OK, gumby, time to get high!

I knew that would grab your attention. It sounds so much more fun than "climbing a boulder." You don't need weed, though—you need a drill sergeant. So…

Get your ass over to the trail! You wanna climb mountains?! My grandmother wants to climb mountains! You're the sorriest little worm I've ever seen! Drop and give me twenty!

Ahem, where were we? Ah, yes. Beginner-level outdoor bouldering consists of (1) finding a surface too steep for a morbidly obese tourist to trudge over, and (2) getting to the top without killing yourself.

Climbing jargon is heavy on "ings." Climb*ing*. Belay*ing*. Rapell*ing*. Fall*ing*. :-o) Dy*ing*. Let's look at your next "ing."

"AW, F#@* IT, DUDE. LET'S GO BOULDERING."

Bouldering is relatively simple. All you need is a crash-pad cushion on the ground to soften your inevitable fall off the boulder, plus a spotter-person to guide your landing. Even better, ask a morbidly obese tourist to help—they'll be your spotter *and* cushion.

How do you find a boulder? Hike the trails of a public park in any state that's not Florida or Illinois. Look for a bunch of people with climbing shoes and chalky fingertips. One of them will be clinging to a rock that's about 10 feet high; the rest are staring at the climber on the pygmy rock. This is a boulder. But it's not *your* boulder, because other people are using it. Keep going until you find a vacant boulder. Stop and wait for your new buddy, the blobby tourist, to catch up.

For some dumb reason, bouldering routes are called "problems." Don't worry—this doesn't mean encounters with tarantulas or black widow spiders (though that could happen). And they're not like equations on a math test you failed. They're way more painful.

Don't you just hate being outclimbed by a 3-year-old?

Common bouldering problems

△ Falling on your head two days after deciding not to buy a helmet.

△ Taking so long to climb the boulder that your spotter elopes with another climber.

△ Feeling your exhausted arms and legs vibrate like a sewing machine needle.

△ Finding raspberry marshmallow Jell-O jammed into a crack.

Let's talk chalk

Hey you! Yeah, you with the powdery palms and the big bucket of chalk you swiped from the climbing gym.

When climbing a boulder, you need only enough chalk to keep your fingertips from slipping. Chalk doesn't increase grip strength or make up for your puny biceps. Don't go flour*ing* your hands and rais*ing* a cloud of dust like an Olympic gymnast.

Chalk does come in handy if you fall off a beginners' boulder and croak when you hit the sidewalk. Investigators might mistake you for a crime victim and use chalk to outline your body. But they'll bring their own chalk. Leave your bucket at home.

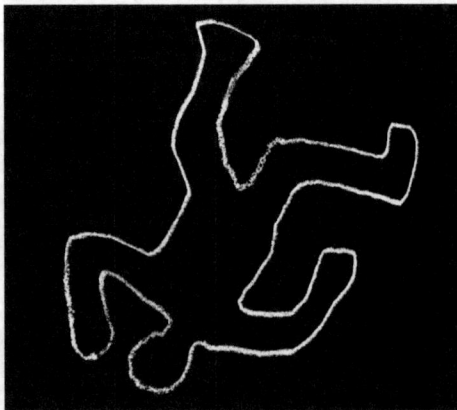

Crime scene or climb scene?

Bouldering skills you don't have yet (and maybe never will)

Great climbers say they "technique" their way up a boulder. My chosen technique would involve an extension ladder, but you can't take shortcuts. You must master balance and movement techniques.

You know those cool balance training boards? The ones with a square platform for your feet and a sturdy half-ball underneath? Don't buy one of those. Even 17 bucks for the cheapest board will be wasted if you give up climbing when the going gets tough, especially if you define *tough* as "getting off the sofa and out the door."

The cheapskate's way to practice balance is to step on and off an unstable surface, like a pile of dirty laundry, or your goldendoodle. Or borrow a pogo stick from a neighbor kid and go bo*ing* bo*ing* bo*ing* around the driveway. If you get really good at pogo*ing*, you might reach the garage roof and get a feel for high altitude.

Fancy footwork

Edging means stepping on a narrow hold with the edge of your shoe. Clever name, huh? Use the inner edge, which will make your big toe howl in protest, or the outer edge, which won't like it either. Meanwhile, your brain is going *This ain't right! Where's the rest of my foothold? Get to a safer place, dimwit!*

Smearing is for when you don't have any foothold at all—just press your sole against the rock as if you're squishing a cockroach. Your brain will go apeshit the first time you even think of smear*ing*. Still, this is what you've gotta do to play with the big boys, as well as that little girl who just climbed around you like a cricket.

Get a move on

You should *keep your feet directly below you*, not splayed out as if you're on a balance beam—or worse yet, directly overhead as you fall off the boulder.

While moving sideways on a route, proper foot placement ensures you don't *barn-door* off the wall. That's worse than the time you left your pants unzipped and the other sixth-graders yelled, "The barn door's open and the horse is getting out!" When climbing, *you're* the barn door, and as you swing, you fall. On the bright side, nobody can see your horse.

Get hip: Pressing one hip against the wall lets you straighten your arms (which relaxes them); holds your weight over your feet (which stabilizes your balance); and makes it look like you know what you're doing (which might impress your three Instagram followers).

There's a popular saying that "Good climbers climb with their eyes." This sounds incredibly painful. Why not your limbs? Hey, there's still time to switch back to bowling.

GOTTA GET GEAR

Shoes, glorious shoes

You're gonna need to buy proper shoes made for bouldering. Consider the lowly gecko. You want shoes that flex, grip, stick, and cling to your back-porch railing. You can train at home and become The Gecko Whisperer.

Now hear this: even if you (and by *you* I mean *you men*) normally would rather die than ask a salesperson for help, get their opinion on climbing shoes. You can almost die of humility now, or certainly die from a fall later on because you tried to climb with ridiculously inappropriate shoes.

Shoes designed for climbing rock walls must fit your foot like a second skin… neon green, incredibly constricting skin. Painfully tight. Every toe, callus, lump and bump should stand out through the uppers.

Flat shoes are flat-soled. Got that? Some soles are hard, the better to help you stand on hairline ledges. Other soles are soft, the better to help you avoid excrutiating pain. Guess which ones you'll like.

Downturned shoes crimp the ball of your foot like the beak of a Red-tailed Hawk diving toward an unsuspecting field mouse. They range from slightly downturned (ouch) to moderately down-turned (owww!) to severely downturned (aaaiiihh!!). They're the workhorses of sport shoes because they fit so many situations, like standing *en pointe* during an impromptu ballet recital.

In a pinch, borrow your sister's ballet shoes.

All these variables create an infinite variety of shoes. Each variety works best in certain situations: smearing on slabs, smearing on smears, toeing into pockets and crimps and crumpets, sticking on steep faces, sticking to catch insects like flypaper, and so on. Because some boulders pose all of these problems, you might end up carrying several dozen pairs in a sling bag or tossing pairs back and forth with your spotter, an advanced bouldering skill known as Tossing Shoes Back and Forth With Your Spotter.

Fancy pants

Don't buy high-performance leggings just yet, because if they help you feel competent, I guarantee you'll get in over your head. But don't show up in baggy jeans, bib overalls or bell-bottoms either, no matter what goofy style is currently popular; everyone will know you're a dweeb. Strike a balance with a pair of flimsy tights from the dollar store.

Bring along a hoodie in case the weather turns crummy while you're waiting for your turn on the boulder. If you ignored my advice about dweeby pants, you'll discover that a dweeb's turn on the boulder comes long after dark. So bring a headlamp, too.

On cold days, wear layers:

- Δ base layer to wick sweat off your skin
- Δ middle layer to wick sweat off the base layer
- Δ outer layer to wick sweat off the middle layer
- Δ a battery-operated fan to disperse sweat from the outer layer toward other climbers. If you're especially putrid they'll take off, and you'll have the boulder all to yourself.

Hill, yeah!

Does the thought of climbing even a lowly boulder give you the cold sweats? Maybe you're feeling peer pressure from friends who have a manic mountain obsession. Maybe you're from Oklahoma, where sensible people avoid high places because tornadoes touch down every five minutes. Maybe you're paranoid about climbing's F-word, which you're supposed to forget.

What you need is a nice, easy hill. You don't climb it—you walk it. The base of your hill might be at sea level. You can walk around the top of your hill without supplemental oxygen. Walk up and down until it starts to feel safe.

The U.S. has plenty of flat states. You can even manage to live in problem states like Colorado (move to the eastern half) and Idaho (southwestern corner).

But maybe that's as far as you'll go. If you breathed a big sigh of relief over this hill concept, you're not cut out for climbing. And we haven't even gotten to techniques of "how to fall." Yes, really.

So drop out, move to Florida, and make new friends whose climbing ambitions never get any higher than Disney's Space Mountain in Orlando.

SKIN IN THE GAME

Shut yer big flap

Skin flaps develop from calluses you're too clueless to deal with. Heck, you take better care of your chalk bag than your hands.

When you climb a boulder, your hands go *Hey, this hurts. Let's thicken the skin.* They keep doing this day after day until your thick skin catches on something sharp, like the corner of a bag of Skittles. The skin tears open, and before you can say "That's a bingo!" you've got a flapper.

Clean up, grease up and bandage that naughty flapper. Swear off long hot baths that turn your skin into a prune; take cold showers instead. And sleep on a bed of nails. Remember that in climbing, agony = authenticity.

Then prevent future flappers. Start sanding down protruding calluses with sandpaper. That's right, sandpaper. This is advice from actual experts, not snarky little me.

Stop using regular moisturizers that make your hands too soft. Buy hand cream that moisturizes the top layer and leaves most of your calluses intact. This specialized cream costs more than Cheapo Creamo from the drugstore because it's made especially for climbers, who are willing to fork over extra cash for everything from specialized climber energy drinks to personalized climber obituaries.

Tape to the rescue

Sometimes it's okay to prevent creepy-callus buildup by taping your hands. For instance, if you work in food service or health care, the customers/patients will scream if you handle their pizza/dislocated finger with your callused monster mitts.

Tape your hands just before a climb, as if you're a bicyclist too cheap to buy proper biking gloves.

After the climb, carefully remove the tape-glove in one piece, as if you're such a cheapsake biker you want to re-use these pseudo-biking gloves. Come to think of it, you could simply cut the fingertips off any old work gloves you have lying around. There, I just saved you a lot of time and money.

Big bruises

So you barn-doored into a rock face, and now your left side is bruised from your ankle to your ass? That's your Purple Badge of Courage, pebble pincher.

The standard medical advice is to elevate the bruised part above heart level, apply a cold pack, and hold it in place for 20 minutes. If you're treating a bruised butt at trailside, this treatment will attract a large crowd and plenty of laughs. Set out a tip jar to make it look like this is all a joke. Which it is.

ATTITUDE ADJUSTMENTS

You've made it pretty far in boot camp. Just to let you know I'm not completely heartless, here are some mistakes you might make at this point, depending on your age. Now you won't have to learn this stuff the hard way.

Wienie teen
What you imagine: Other customers at your local coffeehouse openly admire the beginner's downturned climbing shoes you hobble around in.

What actually happens: Sideways glances. Eye rolls. "Accidental" overcharge for your triple mocha latte.

Twenty-dumbthing
Imagination: Your very first climb draws gasps of amazement from onlookers as you summit in record time.

Reality: Your very first climb draws shrieks of horror as you tumble off the boulder, flattening your spotter-friend.

Midlife-crisis codger
Imagination: You reinvent yourself by purchasing the latest, most expensive clothing endorsed by famous climbers.

Reality: You recalibrate by exchanging all that size-Medium clothing for size-XXL.

Fusty old fart
Imagination: Climbing reveals physical strength you never knew you had.

Reality: You can barely crawl out of bed after exerting muscles you've never used.

Hope for the hopelessly inept

Let's say your heart was set on bagging a dozen 8,000-meter peaks by Labor Day, but you've topped out at 16 inches off the ground on a baby boulder. I hate to break your heart, cupcake—well, actually I enjoy breaking your heart—but you've gotta dial back your ambition.

You still might accompany an 8,000-er climbing party—just not the way you pictured. Every team needs porters, and if you can schlep up a hill with a 50-pound weight on your head, you're in. Don't expect to get any farther than Base Camp, though. The organizers figure you'd crap out with altitude sickness at 5,000 meters, which is roughly the elevation of Denver, Colorado.

Although this porter workaround won't let you rub elbows with the pros, you'll still see those incredible high peaks. Back home, friends might actually look up to you for a change. It's like being a roadie for a rock band, minus the drugs.

One more thought

I'm guessing you got an F in middle school gymnastics. Opponents in high school soccer spiked the ball off your face. If you ever took a Rorschach ink blot test, you probably failed that, too.

What did you do after these failures? Brush yourself off, figure out what went wrong, practice the correct strategy and try again? No, you gave up.

Well, this venture could be different. Go back to the climbing gym, swallow your pride, and ask an instructor for help. Apologize for all those times you left wet towels on the locker room floor. Apologize for leaving mammoth chalk handprints and knee-prints on the wall. Apologize for taking a running start and jumping at the wall like a monkey. (The instructors have a nickname for you, and it's not Sir Edmund Hillary.)

Go back to the beginning of this section, read it again, and take the insults to heart. Eventually, like a lowly caterpillar, you might spin a cocoon. You're not a butterfly yet, just an insect recycling itself in a cocoon. Someday you might even be ready for Part II. But I can't promise anything.

PART II
BASE CAMP: FREAKS AND GEEKS

Habitat: *steep hills, walls of ice, and wilderness areas that can maim or kill you*

Skill level: *good enough to know better, but still too dumb to care*

Somehow you've managed to climb gym walls and easy trailside boulders—but don't pat yourself on the back too long, honey buns. Beyond this point you'll be just another dumb rookie again, with much more at stake.

BASIC ROPE CLIMBING: THE KINDERGARTEN OF MOUNTAIN SPORTS

I can read your mind: "How is basic rope climbing different than what I'm used to?"

1. You're using a rope. Duh.
2. Your upward progress isn't limited to silly little millimeters.
3. You need more equipment than just shoes and chalk. Like, way *way* more. Read on.

Climbing equipment you must buy, borrow or steal

If you're going to be a successful hill climber, you must learn to choose and use lots of specialized gear. If you're going to be an abysmal failure, you'll skip this section.

Helmet: heads up

A climbing helmet helps protect your head in typical situations:

- Δ A rock the size of a microwave oven drops on your skull.
- Δ Failing to look up, you ram into an overhang.
- Δ You miscalculate a side step and bonk your head on a ledge.

Notice that manufacturers claim the helmet will "help" protect your head. If that microwave-size rock falls just right, your head might stay attached to your neck. Makes things easier for the paramedics.

Options include shelled foam helmets vs. hardshell helmets, number of ventilation cutouts, and clips for headlamps and cans of Fat Tire Amber Ale. Replace your helmet if it's riddled with deep dents or when it clashes with the latest Pantone Color of the Year.

Harness: helplessly hanging

When it's time to choose a climbing harness, you'll wish you had a degree in rocket science. If only it were that simple. A climbing harness has more loops, clips and buckles than a six-dog walking leash. If you somehow manage to put it on, you might never get it off.

Manufacturers issue stern warnings for each part of a harness, like "Never hang Christmas lights from this loop!" and "Adjust carefully to avoid cutting off blood supply to your privates!" If that doesn't motivate you to read the directions, nothing will.

During a climb, be careful you don't wind up *inverting*—hanging upside down like a broken puppet—a fatal condition in which you die of embarrassment.

The manly harness men conquer Timm's Hill (elev. 1,951 ft).

Carabiners: your long wait is over

A carabiner is just a humble metal link with a spring-loaded safety closure. But for you it's like a Scouting merit badge. No longer are you a Moron Beginner; you're promoted to an Idiot Beginner. Now you can strut along the trail with a belt that jingle-jangle-jingles like spurs in a classic western movie.

Carabiners come in a dizzying variety of size, strength and weight. Out of billions of options, you absolutely must know these:

1. Wiregate-style carabiners are less likely to vibrate open during a f-f-f-fall.

2. Any carabiner with too little gate-open clearance makes it easier to get your finger stuck in the works.

Whoever dies with the most carabiners wins.

Shop for carabiners at a reputable store. And don't act like you know what you're doing. When the seller asks what kind of climbing you do, be honest: "We've got a 15-foot mulch pile behind our house." (In case you're wondering, they're pronounced *kare ah BEAN ers, kar uh BEAN uhs,* or *kir RIB in eers,* in ascending order of cluelessness.)

One other thought, from Wikipedia: "Carabiners are widely used in rope-intensive activities such as climbing, fall arrest systems… construction, industrial rope work, window cleaning… and acrobatics." It's no coincidence that *climbing* and *fall arrest systems* are listed back-to-back. If this climbing thing doesn't work out, try window cleaning or industrial rope work. Earning a living could turn your life around.

Chalk talk

Were you bummed out when boulder climbing required only a smidgen of chalk? Well cheer up, baby blue eyes, 'cause you're entering Chalk Heaven. Full-hand chalking combats moisture and improves your grip on rock-wall climbs. You'll have pasty white hands, just like the cool boys and girls. You can even apply chalk all over your forearms while wedging into wide cracks. Oh, mercy!

Chalk comes in several forms:

Block chalk, a big hunk of pure chalk, is easy to carry to a climbing spot. Between climbs, keep it on the dashboard to show you're In with the In Crowd.

Loose chalk is… loose. What a coincidence. It comes in fine or coarse grinds, just like those snobby coffee beans you buy.

Liquid chalk comes in a tube. Spread it thoroughly over your fingers and palms until you look like Mickey Mouse. You can make your own liquid chalk with rubbing alcohol, if you don't mind getting dirty looks when you show up smelling like a doctor's office.

Chalk *bags* hold loose chalk: stick your hands inside until they're coated like a Cracker Barrel entrée. Some bags also have a zippered pocket to hold your phone, lip balm and pet gerbil. Chalk *balls* consist of porous fabric with loose chalk inside; dust the ball over your hands. Either method allows you to spill or drop your entire chalk supply at once when you're 100 feet off the ground.

Rope-a-dopes

Dynamic ropes are the kind most people associate with climbing. They're "dynamic" because they stretch, absorbing the impact of a fall. How reassuring—the default rope assumes you're going to fall. If you'd known this earlier, you might have taken up skeet shooting instead.

Who put the "die" in "dynamic ropes"? The makers of cheap ropes, that's who. Quality matters. Do not try to get by with that old tire-swing rope sitting in your garage, unless you want to be immortalized in a YouTube viral video. Buy the best rope you can afford. If you're still living in your parents' basement, buy the best rope they can afford.

Static ropes are used for hauling loads up, lowering injured climbers (you), and lowering other baggage (besides you).

Speaking of loads…
At this stage of your climbing "career" (note the sarcastic quotation marks), you've never been more than 30 vertical feet and 50 horizontal yards away from a public restroom—even if it *is* only one of those gawd-awful pit toilets that hasn't been pumped out since the Civilian Conservation Corps dug it during the Great Depression.

Now, ropes help you climb much higher than 30 feet, which brings us to…

Shit happens

I've been waiting my entire life to use that subhead.

How do climbers poop in mid-climb?

Maybe you hate to think of pooping in public while dangling from a rope hundreds of feet off the ground. Or you're in denial: "Who, me poop? I live on Twinkies and Red Bull."

But consider this: one slip at that height can strike terror into your bowels, making you feel like a commercial for Drano drain cleaner. Unless you've brought sanitary equipment, you'll be forever branded in the climbing community as "Derek the Shitter." Which would be mortifying, especially if your name isn't Derek.

You must carry either a sealable bag or a poop tube. I'm not kidding. A poop tube. Sounds like something a hyperactive second-grader would yell: "Poop tube! Poop tube!" And it gets even better. You can make your own poop tube!

Imagine the joy of stepping into Ace, The Helpful Place, and asking the helpful hardware salespeople where to find PVC plumbing equipment. They'll helpfully ask what size of pipe you need and how you'll use it. You can either mumble and try to shake them off, or be frank about your intentions and watch them helpfully shrink away without turning their back on you.

Instructions for creating your wondrous PVC poop tube are available online. Just don't get them mixed up with videos on making a pipe bomb. Your climbing adventure would be over before it started.

Let's say you're hanging on the wall and have successfully filled your tube. Now you want to get rid of it ASAP. If you've set up a static rope, your belayer buddy can lower the *USS Space-shit* back to earth. Treat that friend like royalty when you're not climbing.

A high-fiber diet is murder on the poop tube.

Let's get back to rope-a-dopes

Most dynamic rock climbing ropes are single ropes. The single rope is perfect for you, the rookie. It's not used with any other rope. That's because it's a single rope. It's used on its own. In case that's not dumbed-down enough, the manufacturer places a circled numeral 1 on either end.

Now that you understand you'll be using a (pop quiz: What kind of rope? A single rope!), you must learn the various lengths and diameters of those (drum roll, please)… single ropes.

Going to great lengths

The 60-meter-long rope has been standard ever since ancient Anasazi warriors climbed to the top of Mesa Verde, took a look at the surrounding desert, and scrambled back down again. Who are you, the raw beginner, to question the wisdom of these tribes? Get a 60-meter rope.

Also note that some modern climbing routes require a 70-meter rope for lowering you to the ground. Do not, *do not*, DO NOT tie a 10-foot clothesline to your 60-meter rope. Also, avoid garage-sale ropes with bloodstains. Your best bet is a brand-new showroom model "starter rope" with a 50-year warranty and optional term life insurance.

Dynamic diameters

OK, take a deep breath. You must also choose the rope's diameter, ranging from 8.5 millimeters to 10.2 millimeters. Doesn't sound like much, yet it's a life-or-death decision. Thinner ropes make it easier for Rookie G. Fumblefingers to tie knots. Thicker ropes are less likely to fray. Would you rather die because of a poorly tied knot or a frayed section? It's your call.

Weaker when wet

An ordinary rope is less stretchy when wet, losing up to 30% of its "dynamic properties." Since you as a beginner have zero dynamic properties, you can't afford even a 1% loss.

Dry-treated ropes are safer. And, like dry-rubbed steaks, they make a delicious snack in mid-climb. Sure, ropes that haven't been dry-treated will regain their strength when they dry out, but who wants to sit in the Laundromat waiting for the dryer cycle to end? Spend extra for the perma-dry style.

Up, up and belay

You're almost ready to climb a genuine outdoor rock face using the technique of *belaying*. It's no coincidence that this sounds like *delaying*: hemming and hawing at the rock wall when you realize you're in way over your head. Belaying has that effect on newbies; make sure your belay device comes with a generous return policy.

Top-rope climbing: now you're getting nowhere

Beginners use the top-rope climbing method, in which the rope passes through an anchor at the top of the hill. *Hmmm.* You're starting at ground level. How did the rope get threaded way up there? Ropes don't thread themselves, so what happened? It's a mystery. Maybe Smokey Bear took care of it for you during a lull in preventing forest fires.

One end of that top-anchored rope attaches to your climbing harness. The belayer-gal/guy standing on the ground feeds the other end of the rope through their belay device. It applies friction to the rope, kind of like the brakes of that car you don't have. The belayer's "braking hand" on the free end of the rope also helps maintain tension.

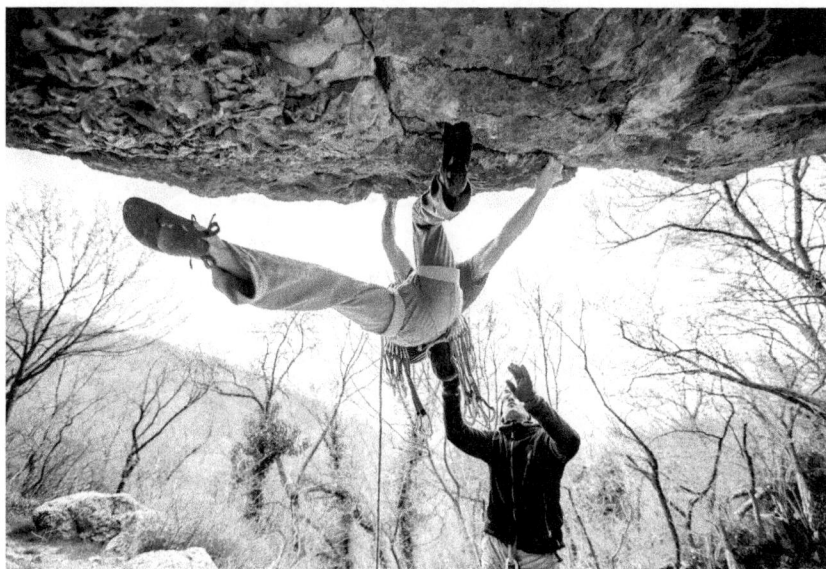

Does your belayer know what he's doing? Probably not.

As you climb, Your Friend the Belayer takes up slack. Keeping the rope taut minimizes the distance you fall each time (dozens) that you slip.

Try to choose a belayer who won't be easily distracted by whatever goes on nearby: a rattlesnake slithers past… some dumb kid drops his ice cream cone on your friend's shoe… an air-raid siren goes off, signaling the start of World War III. You need a partner who pays close attention and understands balance and counterbalance. Or, if you're both a couple of slackers, then hey—whatever happens, happens.

By the way, either/both of you may be stymied by these devices if you have trouble with right & left or up & down. Do people often say "Why are you wearing your shirt inside out?" or "No, your *other* left hand"? You might be better suited to a uni-directional pastime like watching TV.

BELAYING: THE THREE STOOGES METHOD

Climbers

- Δ *Moe:* Tie yourself and Larry to a single top-rope. Climb to the top of the wall. "C'mon, knucklehead! Gimme that ice axe." *CLUNNNNKK.*
- Δ *Larry:* Peer into a large hole in the rock. "Moe, this might be a gold vein." A squirrel bites your nose—you jerk your head back. "Oww!"

Belayer—Curly

- Δ Discover a tangled rope someone left on a rock. "Hey Moe! Hey Larry! Spaghetti!"
- Δ Pull a napkin and fork out of your knapsack ("Nyuk nyuk nyuk!") and let go of the belayer brake.
- Δ Moe and Larry plunge to the ground, landing on top of you and your spaghetti dinner.
- Δ THE END < Cue "Listen to the Mockingbird" jingle >

"What did you say?"
Poor communication during belay climbing increases the risk of confusion, slip-ups, and deadly falls.

Climber: "On belay?" (Ready to belay me?)
Belayer: "What delay?"
Climber: "Eh?"
Belayer: "Yeah, frikkin' A."

Climber: "Climbing." (I'm moving up the hill.)
Belayer: "Climb on." (Go ahead.)

Climber: "Climb on what?"
Belayer: "The rock face."
Climber: "Which place?"
Belayer: "Just climb, for Pete's sake."

Climber: "Give me some slack, Jack!" (Pay out a little rope.)
Belayer: "Can't. I ate all the Cracker Jack. How about some Spam?"
Climber: "I hate Spam."
Belayer: "Try the baked beans, Lobster Thermidor and Spam. It's not got much Spam in it."
Climber: *"Bleecchh."*

Climber: "Tension here." (I'll rest by hanging on the rope.)
Belayer: "Boredom down here."

Climber: "Ready to lower." (I'm done climbing.)
Belayer: "It's about time."

Climber: "Off belay." (I'm standing on the ground next to you.)
Belayer: "Whad'ya think I am, an idiot?"

No wonder Alex Honnold chose free-solo climbing. He didn't have to talk to anyone.

Emergency warnings for falling debris
If you're on the ground belaying and the climber shouts any of these, run like hell.

"Rock!"

"Poop tube!"

"Lobster thermidor!"

"Oh, shit, it's Mr. Creosote!"

Why knot?

You know you're in for a rough ride when basic rope management involves tying a European death knot. Then there's the hangman's noose, the eight-horse hitch, the Believe It or Knot, and the Knot So Fast, Buddy.

Learn to tie knots, they said. It'll be fun, they said.

Somehow you've got to learn this stupefying craft. Your life depends on it. While climbing stores don't sell ready-made knots, they do have instruction books and even reference cards to take along on the hill—which is like carrying a *Student Driver* sign warning other climbers to "Watch out for this dumb flunky."

At times you'll find knotted ropes abandoned at the base of a hill. Did the rope owner manage to walk away? Bad vibes, if you ask me. Leave those knots alone.

Lead climbing: one giant leap for stuntman-kind

Once you've mastered top-rope climbing, you're ready for lead climbing. Ha! You won't bother to master top-rope climbing. You've jumped ahead to lead climbing because it's cool, whereas dangling helplessly from a top rope is definitely un-cool.

Be sure to thank Smokey Bear for his help and tell him you've moved on to lead climbing. He'll try not to laugh—he's heard that one before.

Lead climbing basics

1. You start climbing the wall, clipping your rope into bolts already fixed there (sport climbing) or inserting your own pieces of protection wherever you want them (traditional or "trad" climbing.)

2. Your trusty belayer stands at the base, feeding you slack.

3. In climbing jargon, you're on "the sharp end of the rope"; if that were literally true, you'd somehow manage to spear yourself. Any fall above your last protection-gizmo exponentially increases the risk.

4. So, if you slip when you're five feet above your last cam, you'll fall 5 feet to the cam, another 5 feet until the taut rope is engaged by the cam…

5. …and then 5 times 5 to the 185th power when that cam pops out and all your other poorly placed cams pop out in sequence until finally the rope catches on a secure bolt and launches your itty bitty belayer-person into the stratosphere. Yee-ha!

6. Meanwhile you've plummeted so far into the ground that you won't need burial services. They'll just stick a tombstone next to the hole.

7. Come to think of it, you'd have more fun being the belayer. Be sure to wear a helmet and pack a parachute.

8. So there's your eight basic steps for lead climbing. Have fun!

It's time to hit the climbing store
You: Hi! I need some lead-climbing gear.
Salesperson: (thinking) *Two o'clock. Man, I could be halfway up Deathwish Pass by now.* Sure. What kind of climbing have you done?

You: Oh, just kind of getting a feel for things. *Can she tell I've never been anywhere but the gym?*
Salesperson: This half of the store is all lead-climbing gear. *I think I've got a live one. He needs everything.*

You: Cool! *Uh-oh. Did I bring along the good credit card?*

Coming down (on purpose)

What goes up must come down… ideally, not in 3 seconds or less. Remember our key skills? Coming down in 3 seconds would be fall*ing*. "Climb*ing* good. Fall*ing* bad. Tarzan take Jane to treehouse."

Getting back down the cliff can be more difficult and dangerous than climbing up. The thrill of reaching the summit wears off quickly, and you're tired. You realize how far you've come from the base and look around for an emergency phone to call the park rangers.

Don't count on the rangers; you must safely lower yourself by using your rope to rappel.

Learning the standard rappel technique for self-lowering requires a group class or private lessons. There are plenty of 1,000-step printable instructions online. Trouble is, if you're like me you'd pull out the list, only to have the wind snatch it away, and then what would you do? I'd call my husband, but you can't do that—he's very busy. Get serious about this, lamb chop.

The joy of rapelling: "Don't… look… down…"

CLIMBING'S FOUR-LETTER F-WORD

It's time to revisit climbing's F-word. The one you weren't supposed to remember or imagine. The word you can't get out of your mind. FALL.   :-o

Turns out that there's a right and a wrong way to fall—and no, it's not *fatal* vs. *non-fatal*. After practicing safe falls in a controlled setting, you'll think less about falling and more about climbing. That's the theory, anyway. Personally, I listen closely to my primal fears: falling, tight spaces, spiders, snakes, and people who never shut up. But hey, it's your life. Climbing gurus advise you to push that reasonable, healthy, entirely rational fear of falling out of your mind.

Cut down on foolish falls

Experienced climbers say you must always know where your rope is. It should stay between you and the wall, not over in the next county playing blackjack at the casino. Never let it get behind your legs or wrap around your neck. Ya just cain't trust that lil' sucker.

Before you begin, identify the *crux*—the hardest part—of the route. You'll need to be extra careful when climbing there. If it's a killer route with 10 or more cruxes (*cruxi* is the preferred plural), you have to be extra careful everywhere. Is that even possible? You'd have a lot more fun frittering away your life savings at the casino.

What to call when you fall

- △ Call out "Falling!" so your belayer puts down his peanut butter sandwich and grabs the rope.
- △ Look down at your fall path. Are there ledges or trees in the way? You're screwed.

HAVE AN ICE DAY

As you sink deeper into Obsessive Climbing Disorder, ice climbing might seem like a good idea.

Sane people avoid ice. Or they use it to keep a margarita cold. But deliberately climbing on it? At a steep angle? With hundreds of feet between you and the ground?

OK, if you insist, let's venture into The Wonderful World of Really Hard Water, where you'll learn about 10 zillion kinds of mountain ice, most of them baaaad.

Clear, solid ice at the base of a climb gives you a false sense of security. But at a point where there's no turning back, you hit mushy, crumbling ice. Verglas, a thin sheet clinging to smooth rocks. Rime ice, like the furry stuff in a cheap motel-room freezer. And icicles thicker than your head—which, you must admit, is quite thick indeed.

You're one brittle crack away from becoming a human projectile. You recall what Ralphie's mother told him in *A Christmas Story*: "Those icicles have been known to kill people."

But hey, you asked for it. Ice climbing looked like so much fun as you scrolled through photos of frozen waterfalls on your laptop at home. You remember home, right? That place where you were supposed to be putting up the storm windows or something?

"Look at meeee, I'm as helpless as a kitten up a treeee…"

Get yer ice cold gear here

The ice axe—it's not just for frozen waterfalls anymore! It's also handy on icy terrain when you start sliding backward in slow motion, like Wile E. Coyote. One swing of the Acme Axe arrests your fall—for a few precious seconds. Then the axe breaks off, and that's all she wrote. Final score: mountain 1, you 0.

Sizes and styles vary according to how you'll use the axe:

- △ ice climbing… Do I have to tell you everything?
- △ backpacking on a level trail as you pretend you're training for mountaineering
- △ crossing crevasse fields and snow-covered peaks (in your dreams, kumquat)

You'll also need to buy a leash for your axe. No kidding, a leash. The early days of climbing are like adopting a pet: the animal is only the beginning. In this case it means the ice-axe maker doesn't trust you to hang on to your axe. How well they know you.

I wanna axe you a question: To have or to hold?

You can **secure the axe on your backpack** while driving a half-dozen buddies to the climbing area in your dad's van; drinking beer at the climbing area with buddies; staring straight upward in disbelief from the base with buddies; and daring each other to go first.

You should **carry the axe in your hand** when climbing any angle steeper than five degrees; passing through a bad neighborhood; or pausing on a slippery slope above a crevasse that has your name on it. You must be ready to use the axe the instant you start slipping. This is called self-arrest. In some dodgy neighborhoods crawling with thugs and thieves, that's all the arrest you can count on.

Crampons + you = instant Godzilla

Without crampons, you're not getting anywhere near ice climbing. That's what I would do: not get anywhere near ice climbing. I'd spend that $25, $150, or $275 crampon cash on books, music and fresh flowers. But you're not me, thank goodness, so start shopping for your first pair of crampons right this very minute.

Stick to a reputable sports-outfitting store. You'll need help sorting through all the options:

Δ Bindings that are step-in, strap-on, or lug-bolted to your ankles

Δ 10 points, 12 points, or points numbered to infinity and beyond

Δ Front-point or mono-point; visible or invisible; diurnal, nocturnal or plain old urinal; and with or without "something to drink with that?"

Gnarly crampons turn you into the
meanest S.O.B. on the mountain.

Right away you'll notice that crampons make your boots look beastly, like a mini T-rex. In fact, most crampons come with a care & feeding guide that recommends red meat three times a day. Just make sure the crampons you're wearing don't get too close to your friend's rival brand of crampons. Things could turn ugly.

In addition to climbing frozen waterfalls, crampons let you tackle steep snowdrifts, ascend icy rock-strewn hills, and ruin the uphol-stery of your dad's van when you forget to take them off. They could also help you fight any Arctic wolves you run into, although that might void the manufacturer's warranty.

Now here's where the marketing strategy gets brilliant. Besides crampons, you need gadgets to protect yourself from those cram-pons. It's like buying a fork plus a pair of goggles to keep the fork from plunging into your eye. The basic Crampon Safety Package includes crampon point covers, crampon cases, and gaiters (shin coverings, not swamp creatures).

Everything You Know About Ice Climbing You Learned in Kindergarten

The eensie-weensie climber went up the frozen spout
Down rained the chunks and knocked the climber out
Up woke the climber, who hadn't learned a thing
So the eensie-weensie climber went up the spout again

How to keep climbing when you're not climbing

Though you'd love to hit the hills 24/7/365, sometimes the climbing life is all too much. You're broke, beat up and lonely. You wouldn't mind living out of your car, if you could afford a car. Your parents tell their friends you're deployed overseas. Ever since that last hard fall, your upper body is torqued 45 degrees to the left.

Bummer, dude. Maybe these tactics can tide you over while waiting for your wallet, body and headspace to recover:

Stay connected with climbing buddies by holding a "crap swap." Everyone brings gear they're not using anymore and trades it for gear somebody else isn't using anymore. Yeah, it's still crap, but the grass is always greener on the other side of the mountain. Or the lichen is always greener on the other side of the spire. Something like that.

Create unnecessary risks in your everyday routine for a jolt of adrenaline. If a ceiling lightbulb needs changing, do it blindfolded while balancing on a stack of flimsy plastic crates. Repair a faulty electrical outlet without turning off the circuit breaker.

Give blood on purpose to the Red Cross instead of leaving it on a granite wall. Because when has the wall ever thanked you? Or given you a donut?

A CONFEDERACY OF KLUTZES: WILDERNESS TREKKING

New dynamics come into play with groups of three or more climbers. As the Good Book says, "Where two or three are gathered together, there's a klutz in the midst of them." Or more likely you're all klutzes, bonded by your common klutziness.

Leader of the pack
Who leads the climb? It might be:

△ The person with the most experience, the best judgment or the strongest work ethic. In *your* group? Never mind.

△ Whoever suggested this trip during "last call" at the bar.

△ The only one with a working motor vehicle.

△ Somebody who knows precisely where the trailhead is located (for instance, Colorado).

Whenever possible, you should seize power. The leader decides crucial issues like the timing of potty breaks, who gets the best tent site, and when you should deviate from the trail for lunch at Culver's.

"Is it safe?"
Learn about the weather where you're going. It could be hot as hell, bloody hell, or so foggy you can't see your butt in front of your face. Check long-range weather forecasts online, especially on websites with ads like "Doctors in your area reveal this weird trick for belly fat."

Just before leaving home, phone the visitor center of the park where you plan to climb. Bug the ranger for weather details while she's busy ringing up customers' souvenirs and yelling at kids for climbing the plastic Native American totem pole.

During the climb, order your most nervous camper to keep an eye on the sky. Never mind sailors' superstitions about "red sky at morning." Just tell them to watch for pitch-black walls of cloud, rock-splitting lightning strikes, and hail that strips the leaves from trees. These are indications to seek shelter and start praying.

"One thousand one, one thous—HOLY SHIT!"]

There's nothing random about strikes—lightning really is out to get you. If a direct strike isn't possible, it can jump from a nearby tree, a climbing rope, or your friend's ill-advised fishing pole. Your best bet to avoid lightning injury is to climb with people who are way taller than you.

What you have here is a failure to communicate
Bring reliable communication devices in case your group needs to order an emergency pizza. Remember that even sophisticated methods have their limits. Cellphone batteries go dead. Satellite relays can be jammed by Russian or Chinese hackers. When all else fails, fasten a string between two tin cans and send one can-holder down to the trailhead.

Periodically check that everyone is keeping pace with the group. Count heads. If heads are missing, count limbs. Is everyone carrying a reasonable load, or did the six-year-old collapse under your Yeti cooler? Build time into the schedule for rest stops; insisting that everyone "just hold it" for six to eight hours can trigger a revolt.

"OK, everybody chill."
If people slow to a crawl, your scheduled campsite 50 miles ahead may be unrealistic. Allow them to camp wherever they keel over. Lighten the mood by giving each person an extra marshmallow to roast.

Sometimes Mother Nature provides a blessing in disguise. It starts snowing in the middle of August? Snowball skirmish! The stream that looked so narrow on the map is overflowing its banks? Skinny-dipping party! A record-setting heat wave spoils everything in your picnic sack? Food fight!

Duking it out with hazards
Watch out for common triggers of climbing accidents. One tremendously helpful reference book says the most important rule is "Don't fall." Ah-yup. Then there's "Don't get in the way of a rock slide," "Don't stick your hand in a snake-hole" and "Don't bring a knife to a gunfight."

From bad to worse when it hurts
Despite your best (lame) efforts, accidents happen in the backcountry, just as they do at home: somebody gets stung by a yellowjacket, or develops a toothache, or gets run over by a dump truck while jaywalking. Well, maybe not the dump truck thing. But they could get stung by a yellowjacket, suffer a severe allergic reaction, and develop Mick Jagger Lip Syndrome.

Certain supplies you're already carrying may come in handy for first aid, such as duct tape for a gaping wound. But it's best to bring a dedicated first aid kit. Amazon has some really cool ones in the $200-plus price range. They're so well stocked and official-looking that you could practice medicine next to the pit toilet building.

However, some procedures should never be attempted in the wilderness, including vasectomies and open-heart surgery. And even urgent-med specialists say you should not attempt treatment when (1) there is unacceptable risk to you, the rescuer, or (2) (and I am not making this up) "The patient's body is frozen solid."

At the very least, you should know typical signs of injury:

Δ Bilateral differences—for instance, one side of the torso is fine while the other is only 1/16th of an inch thick.

Δ The victim is screaming bloody murder.

Δ The victim's face looks like it was rearranged by Picasso.

Δ "Cartoon-itis," with double X's where the eyes should be and a spiral shape hovering over the head.

You might have heard of medical conditions related to high-altitude climbing, like AMS, HACE, HAPE, and especially HYPE: claiming you've climbed an 8,000-er when you've never even bagged a 300-yard-er. No worries—you're light years away from high-altitude problems.

You washed your hands in dirty water

How did you pick up a gastrointestinal bug that will give you the runs for months? Let us count the ways.

1. The climbers who previously used your campsite didn't sing "Happy Birthday" while washing their hands.

2. The bear that shits in the woods lives nearby—in which case, your upset tummy is the least of your worries.

3. You forgot to bring biodegradable soap and are washing up with Goo Gone adhesive remover instead.

4. That river where you took a refreshing swim was downstream from a meat rendering plant.

Don't camp here.

Getting ticked off

Ticks are arachnids with really short legs. Since they can't get around quickly, they hitch a ride on your ankle. Crawling north-ward, they might nestle in your nether regions (<*shudder*>) or make it all the way to your scalp. Then they suck your blood, leaving souvenirs like Rocky Mountain Spotted Fever, Lyme disease and Line Dancing Disorder.

Ticks must be removed ASAP. When you set up camp, advise your followers to strip nude for an inspection. To remove a tick, use tweezers and steadily lift outward. Then pull off its legs so it can't hitchhike on someone else. Dirty little bugger.

In case of a panic attack-ack-ack-ack

Climbing steep walls with only a two-inch foothold makes some people nervous. They hyperventilate, seize up, and block the trail. You must prod these sissies to get a move on.

Δ Interrupt the panic cycle by redirecting their attention to some other task. "Can you refill this butane lighter for me?"

Δ Encourage other climbers to provide suggestions and support: "You can do it." "Slow and steady." "Hey, some of us are planning to summit before Christmas!"

Δ Breathing into a paper bag can slow their respiratory rate and restore carbon dioxide levels. Better yet, inhaling laughing gas will have them dancing on the ledge in no time.

SIX SNEAKY STEPS IN CASE OF EMERGENCY

Let's say one of your doofuses manages to break a leg or something. While you may feel sorry for them, your first concern should be to make sure you don't get sued.

Step 1: Be the big gorilla.
Call a meeting with the other climbers. (The broken-leg victim can wait. They're not going anywhere.) Brainstorm to create a mission statement.

Step 2: Deflect blame.
Tell everyone how the victim brought this on themselves by wearing the wrong brand of hiking boots or talking without permission. This distracts your crew from the victim's biggest mistake: trusting you to lead the climb. Assign "action steps" to each person and adjourn the meeting.

Step 3: Get 'em loopy.
Administer your strongest painkillers to the patient. Make sure they understand your reasoning from Step 2. Provide assurance that you've forgiven them and will make their rescue your first priority.

Step 4: Call another meeting.
Ask for progress reports on everyone's action steps. Revisit the mission statement. Break for donuts and coffee.

Step 5: Cover all the bases.
Dictate a Blame Statement elaborating on your points from Step 2. Make sure everyone signs it, especially the victim.

Step 6: Wrap it up.

Assign your brawniest climber to transport the victim to safety using a fireman's carry. Tell the remaining climbers "I guess we could all use a drink, huh?" and break out the first-aid vodka.

BACKCOUNTRY BASICS FOR BOZOS

"Life is either a daring adventure, or nothing."
—HELEN KELLER

"Life is a daring adventure of being ravaged by a pack of wolverines because you're unprepared."
—ME

To survive wilderness climbing, you must make your way over dirt, rock, snow and ice without escalators or pedestrian overpasses. You must spend weeks outdoors without getting swallowed by an anaconda. You must recognize that you've just passed that same huge boulder for the fifth time in three days.

Ready, steady, think
Can you sustain a thought for 10 seconds without consulting your cellphone? Do you know what an approaching blizzard looks like? Do you even know what the sky looks like? Would you freak out if a guy speared himself with his own crampons and started bleeding like a stuck pig?

Another cellphone-related climbing death.

Get your goofball act together

"I don't even have any good skills. You know, like nunchuck skills, bow hunting skills, computer hacking skills. Girls only want boyfriends who have great skills!"
—NAPOLEON DYNAMITE

To put this in Napoleon-ese, you need to solve backcountry problems like rock slides, volcanic eruptions, rabid porcupines, and hissy fits among climbing companions. If you solve these problems successfully, you survive.

Way to go! Now you have a few survival skills. You won't get to use them on future outings, though, because the wilderness throws new problems at you each time. That's why it's so addictive, like pulling your own hair.

The No-Nitwit Code of Conduct
By avoiding nitwitty behavior, you'll save yourself lots of hassles and embarrassment.

1. Leave a copy of your itinerary at the nearest ranger station. They could use a good laugh.
2. There should be at least three people in your climbing party. Five or more is even better. You're going to lose a few to predators, boredom, and hookups with good-looking climbers in other groups.
3. Rope up on any incline over zero degrees.
4. When facing a difficult judgment call over safety concerns, ask yourself, "What would Scooby Do?"

STOP WHINING AND START PACKING: 10 ESSENTIALS

You're not just woefully unprepared—you're *predictably* unpre-pared. Barely five minutes past the trailhead, you'll start bleating like a lost lamb. This list anticipates the top 10 bleats and helps you avoid them, decreasing the risk of mutiny by your climbing party.

1. *"Where the heck am I?" (navigation aids)*

- Δ   Take *maps:* trail maps, topographic (elevation) maps, road maps, and brochures showing Hooters locations in all 50 states.

- Δ   A *compass* shows you which way to hold the map so you don't lead your group to Decatur, Illinois, the Soybean Capital of the World.

- Δ   An *altimeter* explains why you're feeling that Rocky Mountain high.

- Δ   *GPS devices* (e.g., Ms. Google Maps) provide an excuse to look at your cellphone.

- Δ   A *personal locator beacon* produces an electronic scream for help when all of the above fail.

2. *"I can't see a thing." (nighttime illumination)*

Get a *headlamp* that has both a wide beam to illuminate the trail and a spot beam to locate the rock that tripped you anyway, so you can kick and swear at it. Take plenty of extra *batteries;* your buddies will need them, and you can issue exhorbitant IOU's that will more than pay for all your new equipment.

3. "I'm burnt to a crisp." (sun protection)
Quality *sunglasses* protect your eyes from harmful radiation and give you that Joe Cool vibe. Quality *SPF clothing,* like a wide-brimmed hat and a loose white shirt with an upturned collar, suggests you just dropped in from a walkabout of the Australian outback. And quality *sunscreen* maintains your attractiveness for years to come, because there's no such thing as sexy skin cancer.

4. "I feel like crap." (first aid)
The novice's variation of Murphy's Law states, "Anything that can go wrong will go wrong, and it will be your fault." As I've already told you, beanbag, take a complete first-aid kit. Or a bare-bones kit. Or just a couple of old crumpled Band-Aids at the bottom of your snack tote.

5. "How the heck can I fix this?" (small tools)
So many things can happen that a rolling eight-drawer mechanic's cabinet would really come in handy. At the very least, bring safety pins, seam ripper, iron-on hem tape, and knives. Especially knives. Even a simple butter knife can serve as a cutter, screwdriver and weapon.

6. "My water bottle leaked onto the matches." (fire starters)
You must get a good fire going to roast the cornish hen and perform your lame version of the Apache fire dance. Forget matches—pack a small butane lighter and chemical firestarters. Also, a fire extinguisher helps avoid a catastrophic forest burn that would become known as Derek the Shitter's Camp Fire.

7. "It's frikkin' freezing out here, Mr. Bigglesworth." (emergency shelter)
Which will you carry: a survival blanket, an insulated tarp, a thermal bivy? Or a jumbo plastic trash bag?

8. "We're all gonna starve." (extra food)

If anything delays your return to civilization, you'll need extra food that's easy to glom down in handfuls, like Tostitos, Spaghetti-Os and other health food ending in "Os." Pack extra coffee to keep your caffeine junkies from morphing into Edvard Munch's "The Scream." If your group is truly famished, instruct them to scavange for earthworms and dung beetles; organic-food proponents recommend these delicacies for their protein content and satisfying mouthfeel.

Mmm, dung beetles. Betcha can't eat just one.

9. "We're all gonna die of thirst." (extra water)

A gallon jug of water weighs a whopping 8 pounds. Tell your most macho climbers that trekking with a jug in each hand makes a great upper-body workout. Once your original stockpile runs out, locate reliable sources like lakes, rivers and water-bottle vending machines in pristine mountain meadows (bring dollar bills). Don't fall for the old myth about drinking urine, either your own or someone else's. That actually speeds up dehydration, especially if it makes you puke.

10. "I have no idea what to do next." (mountain mastery)
Take this book along. Bring copies for your fellow climbers, too. Between the three, four, five or whatever of you, that could add up to a single well-informed brain.

Buy now or regret later

You'll also need a decent sleeping bag, a high-quality tent and an appropriate camping cookstove. If your first overnighter involved slurping down cold ramen noodles and sleeping unsheltered on a rock, that would probably be your last overnighter. And you'll have bought this book for nothing.

It's in the bag
"Nighty-night, sleep tight" is literally true with the standard mummy bag, which doubles as a spooky King Tut costume on Halloween. Some climbers choose to camp "ultralight" with only the mummy bag and no tent, yet going without shelter leaves you more vulnerable to predators. Maybe you should sleep with your dog, who will burst into a frenzy of precautionary barking as you get mauled by a bear.

Basic mummy bag (cute mutt not included).

As a beginner, you're better off with a regular sleeping bag. These use either synthetic fiber or natural down. Synthetic fiber, usually polyester, dries quickly and insulates even when wet—like when you foolishly sleep under a tree, guaranteeing that raindrops keep fallin' on your head long after the storm has passed.

Natural down is the insulation of choice for cold, dry conditions, such as a walk-in beer freezer at the liquor store. Make sure the down came from geese or ducks that were humanely treated. Look for product labels certifying basic freedoms of animal welfare, including freedom from want, freedom from fear, and freedom of expression ("Aflac! Aflac! AFFFLAAAACKKK!")

Manufacturers rate the efficiency of sleeping bags for a "standard man" or a "standard woman." You, as a substandard man or woman, may simply choose whatever color you like. Don't get hung up on optional features like motorized massagers and mosquito repellent coils, since it's too early to guess what'll work for you. Grab whatever's on sale, then use it during your first few overnights to discover what you hate about it.

To stay warm in your sleeping bag, ask a seductive climber to join you, eat Carolina Reaper peppers as your bedtime snack, and tuck a hot-water bottle inside your jammies.

There's also the modest bivy sack, hugging you like the paper around a Jimmy John's Thai Chicken Wrap. You might envy climbers who get by with just the bivy shell and no sleeping bag. Don't try this. I can hear you whining already.

Cushion yourself from the hard ground with a closed-cell foam mat or self-inflating pad. Or, since you're the leader, simply order everybody to surrender their jackets and spread them out under your bag.

A-TENT-shun!

"Be it ever so humble, there's no place like a tent" said no one, ever. But you've gotta sleep somewhere, and the tent shelters you from weather and gives you a little privacy to do, uh, whatever it is you do to fall asleep.

A substandard person exhales lots of moisture. Open all vents and windows, allowing your tent to "breathe." You also give off gallons of perspiration when ultra-insulated in clothing, sleeping bag and camp blanket; peel these off and sleep in the nude. How will your fellow campers react to this combination of nudity and wide-open tenting? It depends on your physique.

Of course there's a billion-and-one tent options: dome tents, four-season tents, fly tents, and tents with hardwood floors and oodles of closet space. As with any gear, you must strike a balance between a tent's features vs. how much weight your servants are willing to bear.

With so many choices, it's impossible for me to explain the setup process for your particular tent. Here's an overall rule for you guy campers (gals already know this):

Read the freakin' instructions!

CAMP STOVES: A PAIN IN THE GAS

If you think camping is a simple way to reconnect with nature, camp stoves are here to mess with your mind. Like a typical rookie, you buy a dirt-cheap product from a dicey internet seller offering *Great campering cookstove make your outdoor meals like gourmay*. This crapstove repeatedly malfunctions until you're so fed up that you smash it to pieces with a tree branch. Then you remember that civilized substitutes at outdoor-gear stores, True Value Hardware and Chick-fil-A are at least a four-day hike away.

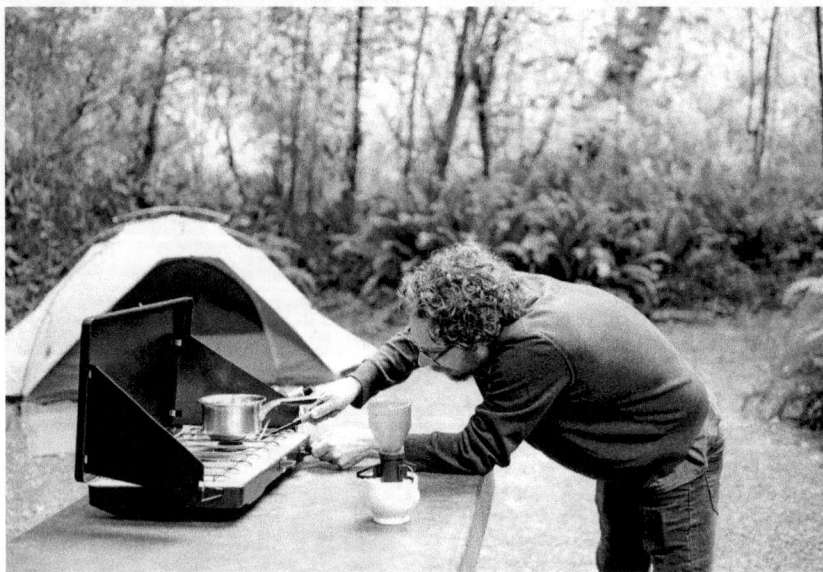

"Dag-nabbit stupid razzle frazzle junky stove!"

Well, in the meantime, unless the fire danger level in your area is Crayola Burnt Sienna—"EXTREME. No outdoor burning allowed ever, anywhere. This means you, punk."—you can build a good ol' cowboy fire by gathering dry leaves, brush and logs. Watch the flames flicker while somebody plays mournful songs on a harmonica. It really makes you nostalgic, even if your idea of the good old days resembles the fart scene in "Blazing Saddles."

Water, water everywhere

Most experts agree that you should drink water. Those who disagree are dead or banished from the climbing community. No doubt you've heard that darker urine means you're dehydrated. It can also be a sign of pregnancy, diabetes or kidney disease, which gives you something to worry about in your tent overnight, besides bears.

Assume that every backcountry water source is loaded with parasites, protozoa, and other pathogens, all of which start with "p." Yet most chemical water-treatment options sound awfully drastic. Chlorine dioxide? Iodine?!

Luckily, you can kill all those p-p-pathogens just by boiling your water. Then use a filter to strain out wasps, stones and other stuff you p-p-probably don't want to swallow.

Purina Climber Chow

By planning ahead, you can choose nutritious foods that won't spoil and don't weigh too much in your backpack. Or, by wandering the grocery aisles when you're hungry, you can find stuff you *really* want, like pizza burgers, pork butt, a dozen kinds of cheesy chips, cupcakes, and gallon jugs of sugary drinks. After all, you'll burn anywhere from 4,000 to 5,000 calories per day. In fact, nutritionists say you should never diet while climbing! You've found your perfect sport!

And there's more good news: it's best to consume **carbohydrates** steadily as you climb. Which means you don't have to change your usual daily habit of scarfing down cake, donuts and sugary cereal without pausing for breath. The only difference is that now you're walking instead of lounging in your recliner.

Before too long you'll find a cadence that lets you fill your mouth every time you swing your dominant hand.

Protein-rich foods range from those you love (peanut butter, cheese, canned meat) to those you wouldn't touch if you were starving (powdered milk, tofu). Foods that provide **fat** are your dream menu: potato chips, salami, butter, butter, and butter.

Some campers buy a food dehydrator to prepare healthful items that are easy to pack. Does the term "fruit leather" sound appetizing? If not, you just saved yourself $159.

The right cookpot can make any meal inedible.

Another thing: Never volunteer to coordinate meals for your group. One person won't eat meat, one freaks out over sugar, another insists on organic-everything, and still another could die if any ingredient came within 100 miles of a peanut.

Don't forget to bring lightweight bowls and spoons, unless your group has gone native with everybody sticking their hands in the cookpot. And if you enjoy cooking, stay away from tempting camp-cookware offerings like portable espresso makers, air fryers and pressure cookers. Jeez Louise, you're climbing a mountain. Why don't you bring a piano while you're at it?

When you're too high to cook
In the extremely unlikely event that you ever climb above 10,000 feet, be aware that altitude sickness causes headaches, nausea and delusions of competence. Plan to eat small amounts of light foods, like the rice with cooked chicken the vet recommends when your dog has swallowed another tennis ball.

Move your keister
Wilderness travel becomes risky when you're in a mental state of bewildered-ness. Gather as much information as possible from guidebooks, maps, forest service agencies, and that sexy park ranger in the visitor center (ask for their phone number and the time they get off work.)

Then, just get going. Even the best planning guides have their limits, so maintain a keen eye, a sharp ear and a forked tongue.

Be flexible. If the route you've chosen has been obliterated by a meteorite, choose another path. And always give yourself the option of an early return (a.k.a. bailing out). Whether or not you share this plan with your climbing party is up to you. If it involves parachuting over a cliff and you have the only parachute, mum's the word.

Hiking with your groupies
A big part of mountain climbing is just plain old walking. Some mountaineering books even tell you how to walk: when to inhale or exhale when either foot is in front, whether to look up or straight ahead, how to hold your hiking pole, and so on. All I can say is: if you're that clueless, stay home.

Leading a hike means keeping everybody together, from the slowest beginner to the most impatient veteran climber. Ha. Good luck with that. Here are some strategies to use if you feel like it.

△ Try to keep all your people in the same climate zone.

△ When you must stop, get your ass off the trail so others can continue.

△ If your party encounters pack animals, step aside quietly and let them go by. Then grab the weakest one at the back and slaughter it for supper.

△ Make that gung-ho experienced climber carry the food dehydrator.

△ If you encounter a bear or a wildcat, speak softly yet assertively: "Say there, cougar. How's your day going so far?" Slowly back away until there's a larger and more appetizing hiker between you and the wild thing.

△ Never admit that you've lost the trail. Pick up the pace and surge ahead.

The flip side

Up to this point I've assumed you couldn't care less what the other climbers think of your leadership. But what if you really *do* give a rat's patooty? Maybe you want to become a professional guide someday. Or you're angling for a cash tip when the outing is over.

In that case, take your cues from today's leading hospitality experts: focus on "the client experience."

Hire a celebrity chef to create farm-to-mountain menus with hormone-free meat, line-caught fish and locally sourced fruit and vegetables. Provide nightly turndown service with a gourmet chocolate on each sleeping bag pillow. Conduct exit interviews; as the Medevac helicopter hovers overhead, ask the injured climber, "On a scale of one to 10, how would you rate today's rescue from the rockslide?"

THE DIRTY LOWDOWN ON CAMPSITES

Despite your incompetence, everybody survived day one of the trek? Congratulations! Now you have a whole new set of problems!

Location, location, lousy location

There are no perfect campsites; some just suck less than others. One campsite with plenty of flat space suitable for tents is infested with clouds of mosquitos. Another, perched next to a sparkling mountain stream, has been overrun with poison ivy. A beautiful forest site is so damp your clothes turn moldy within minutes.

So get ready to put up with musty odors, muddy water and hordes of flying pests. Good ol' boring safety must come first: Avoid camping in high-crime neighborhoods, leper colonies, sinkholes, sanitary sewers, active volcanoes and tornado alleys.

"And they call the wind… wind"

Pay attention to prevailing wind direction. Strong gusts can pick up your tent while you're in it and dash you against a rock wall. That might be fun if you're a teen accustomed to thrill rides at Six Flags. If not, you'll prefer an earthbound tent.

According to experts, you should:
…place the tent door into the wind to minimize the constant flap-flap-flapping that drives climbers nuts.
…place the door away from the wind to keep out rain and snow.
…set up the side with the strongest pole structure facing into the wind.

As you can tell, experts are even more confused than you are. Since you'll be pitching your tent for the first time ever, probably after dark in driving rain or snow, just get the dang thing set up any way you can and crawl in.

No food left behind for wildlife

Don't bring food into the tent, where other campers will tear everything apart to get at it. And never, never, never feed wildlife. You know what they say: "A fed bear is a dead bear." Especially if it eats that fruit leather your hippie friend brought along. If Mr. Bear survives the fruit leather, you'll have 500 pounds of irate revenge with tooth and claws coming after you.

Winter camping? Give me a break!

Having endured way too many harsh winters in the Upper Midwest, I believe the use of *snow* and *camping* in the same sentence indicates an unhinged mind.

Those mountains you hope to climb someday aren't getting any shorter. Snow is inevitable. But winter camping just for the sake of winter camping at lower elevations? Bah, humbug.

Winter camping—what's the point?

Let's take a flying leap in the opposite direction:

Car camping—what a relief!

Cowering inside a tent way out in some godforsaken creepy wild place isn't for everyone. Why not camp in your car? Just imagine relaxing in a cocoon of metal and glass on a U.S. Forest Service road or Bureau of Land Management area. Or parked at the trailhead. Or at the nearest Walmart with restrooms open 24 hours a day.

As a solo or two-person venture, car camping won't add any leadership credentials to your resume. But that's more than outweighed by its many advantages.

△ Your car won't blow away in the wind, and you'll never be bugged by any flap-flap-flapping of tent fabric.

△ If a lightning storm moves in, you're far less likely to be zapped to a crisp.

△ You can bring all kinds of camping furniture without carrying any of it on your back. Folding table and chairs. Solar-powered washer and dryer. Wide-screen high-def TV.

△ Bring your pets. A strenuous climb to reach a tent campground wouldn't be fun for your iguana, and your dog is even lazier than you are. But they'll love a road trip.

△ Since your car just sits there all day and you must return to it at nightfall, you have a solid excuse to do minimal climbing. Or none at all.

△ You don't need to bear-proof your food provisions at night—just make sure the doors and windows are locked. Then watch Mr. Bear gazing and drooling at the forbidden food. Stick out your tongue at him.

LEAVE SOME DEBRIS: A REALISTIC GUIDE FOR SELFISH TREKKING

The trailhead signs implored you to "Leave No Trace," but instead…

△ You camped atop a nice soft surface of alpine flowers that took 158 years to grow five inches, and now are dead.

△ You made record time by cutting a dozen switchbacks on the trail.

△ Your favorite souvenir from Glacier National Park is the endangered Plotkin's ground squirrel that you caught, brought home, and had stuffed and mounted by a taxidermist.

While growing up, you never had to make your bed or shovel out a path to the desk. You probably weren't toilet-trained until middle school. The one and only time you cut the lawn with Dad's riding mower, you destroyed his hydrangea bushes.

Let's face it, you'll never bother to Leave No Trace. For you, Leave Some Debris (LSD) might be achievable. Here's how this plays out in the real world.

Manage human waste
Leave No Trace Instead of toilet paper, use smooth stones, snow or pine cones.
Leave Some Debris Use a page of that thriller you're reading. It's not very interesting anyway.

Preserve vegetation
LNT Leave plants, rocks and other natural features alone. Draw or photograph them if you want a keepsake.
LSD Well, maybe just pick a few of those spiky purple flowers.

Handling food and garbage
LNT Carry out any leftover food.
LSD Eat all leftovers.

This isn't my idea of toilet paper.

LNT Clean cooking utensils at least 200 feet away from water sources. Dig a cat hole to dispose of grey water.
LSD Carry a 50-pound seasoned cast iron skillet that never needs washing.

Encourage a love of nature among tomorrow's campers
LNT Lead the Junior Rangers club on a deep-woods hike to identify wild-bird calls and chattering squirrels.
LSD Inspire future smartasses with a YouTube video of the original Alvin and the Chipmunks singing "Japanese Banana."

Respect wildlife

LNT Don't bring along pets that will disturb native mammals and birds.

LSD "But they won't mind my boa constrictor, right?"

LNT Don't get too close to wild creatures.

LSD "Heeerre, Two Socks. That's a nice wolf. Want some cheese?"

PART III
SUMMIT: HARDCORES

Habitat: You're on Mountain Time, confronting knife-edge
   ridgelines, tops of peaks, bottoms of crevasses, and middles of
   avalanches.

Skill level: superb—but Fate doesn't give a damn.

You're becoming an elite mountaineer, a high-stakes game in
which every move could be your last. You've abandoned your job,
your home, maybe even your family—which leaves you free to do
nothing but climb… climb… climb… climb.

Let's see what you're getting into, potential peakbagger.

A WHO'S WHO OF MOUNTAINS

You've dreamed of mountains ever since you took your first baby steps, climbed a kitchen chair, fell off and cracked your noggin. Climbing can be agony *and* ecstasy: those seductive peaks will stab you in the back.

Are you ready? These aren't just scenes in a movie. Every mountain has its own climate, personality and homicidal intent.

Mont Blanc, the ultimate tourist trap

Its handy location on the border between Italy and France lures novice climbers to Mont Blanc, which returns the favor by killing them. Mont Blanc has snuffed out more people—8,000 and counting—than any other mountain. That's a lotta dead newbies. Might be a good place for you to start.

North Face of the Eiger: the Super Bowl of mountaineering

The North Face. It dominates books, photos, films and your fevered mind. Hordes of people at the base watch intently, as if your climb is the Super Bowl. Some root for you to win. Others secretly hope the game goes into sudden death overtime.

Alpamayo: ice ice baby

This beautiful, frigid ice queen beckons you to summit her. Just don't tell your wife.

Annapurna, Public Enemy #1

Annapurna punches above its weight. The 10th highest peak in the world, it boasts a 40% summit fatality rate, which means a mountaineer is more likely to die here than on any other 8,000-meter climb. It's just what you've been dreaming of.

Everest, the mountain we love to hate

Everest is the McDonald's of high peaks: crowded, overly familiar, dumbed down for mass consumption. It's only a matter of time before somebody starts running luxury motorcoach tours to the summit.

K2, Everest's evil twin

If Everest is a tourist resort, K2 is a battle zone. Climber George Bell called it "a savage mountain that tries to kill you." Only 820 feet shorter than Everest, it's really pissed off at being ranked #2.

"Everybody got their picnic lunch?
We'll summit K2 by noon!"

Denali: unleash your inner pack animal

If your idea of fun involves dragging 150 pounds of food and gear on a sled from Base Camp to Camp 1, then have at it. Or maybe the mere thought has you fuming: "My mama didn't raise no donkey."

Baintha Brakk, for the hardest of the hardcore only

Nicknamed The Ogre, steep and rocky Baintha Brakk defeats even the best mountaineers. Never mind a living will—just make sure your basic dying will is in order before strapping on your crampons for the double-B.

Kangchenjunga: there will be blood

"If you mention back at the office that you've spent two months climbing a peak called "K-A-N-G C-H-E-N J-U-N-G A", you'll get a 'whaaaat???'" wrote Dutch mountaineering expert Peter Boogaard. On the other hand, "the entire history of the mountain is spilled with blood," so it might be worth your while.

Kang Guru: not a warm & fuzzy marsupial, mate

The Himalayan peak of Kang Guru lures you close with a cuddly baby mountain in its pouch, then punches, kicks and bites. Crikey!

NEXT STOP: THE DEATH ZONE

Oh-so-noble alpine-style climbing

Alpine purists define themselves by negatives: no network of fixed ropes, no Sherpas, no well-stocked camps en route, no ferrying of supplies up and down the mountain, and no $10,000 official expedition wristwatch as worn by Daniel Craig in "James Bond: No Time to Retire."

Your backpack must hold every piece of your equipment, food and shelter. Rookies always underestimate how much food they need and overestimate how much equipment to bring; you'll be starving as you throw away excess supplies. But since you enjoy suffering, it's all good.

Benefits of alpine climbing vs. expedition climbing:

- Δ cheaper
- Δ faster
- Δ Nobody will check your mountain climbing credentials.

Drawbacks of alpine style:

- Δ Nobody will discover that you *have* no mountain climbing credentials and might croak while stepping off the plane in Nepal.
- Δ If you're caught in a blizzard after ditching too much gear, you'll have to use your undies as a bivy sack.
- Δ The need to navigate on your own is a deal-killer if you still use Ms. Google to find your way home from Publix.

And now for the 800-pound gorilla:

Uber-gonzo expedition-style climbing

Expedition outfits lay siege to a mountain with all the subtlety and finesse of Genghis Khan and the Mongol Horde. Climbers travel up and down a fixed line to multiple camps, gradually adjusting to high altitude and then zoning out in the Base Camp's plunge pool.

Expeditions bring everything *and* the kitchen sink. Way back in 1950, Maurice Herzog's team made the first summit of Annapurna with:

- △ 56 French climbers
- △ 278 Sherpas (scaled down from 452 after their customary strike)
- △ 25,000 pieces of equipment, including two undermount sinks
- △ three horses and a camel
- △ 117 bottles of fine wine
- △ 250 cartons of cigarettes

Expedition climbing enables everybody and their freakin' cousin to try big mountains: Girl Scout troops, librarians, convicted felons, quilters, clowns—and you.

Let's hear it for the Sherpas

Sherpas are a Nepalese ethnic group renowned for their climbing skills and endurance at high altitude. Without professional climbing Sherpas, there would be no expeditions.

They place ladders and fix ropes over dangerous sections of the route. They set up camps and make sure hot tea is ready when clients need it. They keep a straight face when clients ask for a Starbucks latte. When severe weather keeps everyone confined to tents, they hand out bingo cards and set up Twister mats.

The Death Zone: "The Grim Reaper will see you now."

Climb high enough and you'll encounter the Death Zone, where oxygen is too limited to sustain human life. You'll find the Big DeeZee on any summit above 8,000 meters (26,000 feet)—the height of the climbing community's 14 most-wanted peaks. "Any of those mountains can kill me? Let's go, bro!"

In the Death Zone, your brain swells. Judgment is impaired—you might decide to throw away your ice axe or buy a timeshare in Phoenix. Your heart races. Cells begin to die. Your whole life flashes before your eyes, and you regret spending so much quality time with the kids when you could have been climbing the corporate ladder.

The most prestigious peaks reside in the Himalayan and Karakoram mountain ranges of Nepal, Tibet and Pakistan. Envious first-world countries have petitioned the United Nations to let them annex several of the best mountains—but so far, no dice.

To climb in this high-class neighborhood, you'll need a permit. To get a permit, you'll need an expedition. To get an expedition, you'll need some climbing references and a boatload of cash. If you don't have legitimate references, you'll need another boatload of cash to buy some shady references.

WHAT TO EXPECT WHEN YOU'RE EVEREST-ING

Most likely your first big-mountain attempt will be Everest. Despite its notorious climbing tragedies, somehow you believe Everest will be relatively easy (it won't), climbers of all teams and nationalities willingly cooperate (they don't), and your team leaders will always be nearby to hold your hand (they can't).

"I paid $60,000, and there's not even a Porta-John at Base Camp?"

Say goodbye to privacy. At Base Camp you'll use the bathroom tent when nature calls. Later you'll realize that this makeshift restroom was a luxury. During the climb you must open the built-in seat flap of your pants and crouch on the ground with snow glomming onto your bum. If you need to pee at night without leaving the tent, you use your own bottle—and *not* a Gatorade bottle, even if you're fond of practical jokes.

This expedition may be your first encounter with the sport's big guys and gals who have millions of social media followers. Their bags and clothing are plastered with sponsors' logos. If you're lucky, maybe your neighborhood dollar store will chip in a few bucks to place their logo on your butt flap.

Hints that you're hindering

Don't clog the trail, doorknob. If a huge line forms behind you, step aside to let others go ahead. There might be hundreds of "others," so be patient. Make believe you're at Universal Orlando without an express pass.

Maybe, by some miracle, you'll find yourself keeping up with a faster group. In that case you can borrow from golf etiquette when you encounter slower climbers: "Mind if we climb through?" But don't look smug. You might run into these same climbers on your way back, when you're desperate for a hit from their oxygen supply.

Crumping

At some point the difficulty and danger of Everest will get to you. You couldn't care less about continuing the climb; you just want to go home. This is known as "crumping."

Invent some crump excuses in advance. You could say your wife burned down the house in a desperate bid for attention. Or your boss is suspicious because you've been calling in sick with the same head cold for two months. Come to think of it, those excuses are probably legit.

The trouble is, giving up now would put you in a real bind. Just think of how much non-refundable dough you paid for this idiotic trip. And if you drop out, the yak-rental agency won't accept your travel rewards credit card for a lift back to civilization.

So just keep climbing until you keel over from altitude sickness. Now *that's* crumping.

Fun features of Everest

The Khumbu Icefall—highway to hell

Khumbu Ladders & More in Kathmandu has a 50-year sponsorship deal giving it naming rights to the Khumbu Glacier and the notorious Khumbu Icefall, a jumble of huge frozen Lego bricks at the head of the glacier.

As the Icefall's seracs (ice towers) constantly shift and collapse, Sherpas determine the best route and place KL&M's ladders across yawning crevasses. Then comes the really fun part in which you adjust to high altitude by crossing this deadly route *several times*, back and forth between higher elevations and Base Camp, in a process known as "torture."

Ambitious climbers recently found an alternate route that avoids the Icefall. If this detour opens to expeditions, a toll scanner will verify a microchip in your forehead as you wheeze on by.

The Khumbu Icefall: Everest's shitty welcome mat

The Western Cwm—one big honkin' gorge

Cwm (pronounced "koomb") is a Welch word for "don'tcha climb there, lad." *Cwoom* was the original name; the glacier scraped off its vowels.

Khumbu Ladders & More has a franchise here, too, which means—you guessed it—more crevasses! Did you know that you can earn Khumbu Kash every time you cross a crevasse on one of KL&M's ladders? Just apply for a Frequent Crosser Card. The nearest Sherpa will credit your account as you navigate each ladder. Then spend your Kash on yak-hair sweaters, tea pots, alpaca butter and more.*

Some restrictions apply. Kash not eligible toward purchases of name-brand climbing wear, boots, crampons or tents. Offer is subject to availability and acts of God, including blizzards and avalanches. No rain checks or snow checks. Not transferable to others after climber's demise.

The South Col—where Everest dreams go to die

Your final camp before the summit lies at the South Col. On this pass between Everest and Lhotse (the world's fourth-highest mountain), high winds scour away snow cover and climbers.

At its 25,938-foot elevation, the Col is just a field of rocks with a sign proclaiming "Gateway to the Death Zone." You've gambled an extraordinary amount of money and effort to roll the weather dice. If you don't reach the summit in two or three days, the alien atmosphere will turn you into a pumpkin.

Keep an eye out for "Mr. Hustle" Sherpa, who earns tips by taking photos of climbers in front of the Death Zone sign. He also sells souvenir t-shirts that say "I almost summited Everest."

The former Hillary Step

No doubt you've obsessed over classic tales of historic first summits, complete with dire accounts of the notorious Hillary Step: a nearly vertical 40-foot rock face, the last big obstacle before the peak. You reach it when you're totally wasted after 12 solid hours of climbing. Even worse, getting past the step requires advanced technical skills. For first-timers like you, they use a horse sling with ropes and pulleys.

But now for some really good news. Sometime before 2017, the Hillary Step disappeared! All that's left is a gradual snowy slope. Nobody knows where the Step went. Was it kidnapped? Did it move to Shanghai? Maybe it just got tired of being cussed at and stepped on, and quietly took an early retirement.

At any rate, local Sherpas opened the 2019 climbing season with a ribbon-cutting ceremony proclaiming it The Step Formerly Known as Hillary.

The original step was named after Sir Edmund Hillary, the first to reach Everest's summit in 1953, along with Sherpa Tenzing Norgay. Let's hope they're not spinning in their graves over this downgrade.

Ex-climbers—the most ghastly feature of Everest

Not everyone makes it to the summit, and not everyone makes it back to Base Camp, ever. Climber cadavers are a permanent part of the landscape because it's too risky for others to make their way down the mountain carrying a dead weight (literally).

The Sherpas, for their part, don't have to decide whether it's safe; they believe that moving the dead brings misfortune. Smart Sherpas.

The tent life ain't no good life

What's it like to cram into a tent at 24,000 feet with too many other climbers? Check out these entries from their diaries.

> *"…smells like a pigsty. Nobody has showered for a month."*
>
> *"Everything covered with ice. So cold I can hardly think. My pencil is cracki…"*
>
> *"I've seen coffins bigger than this tent"*
>
> *"so tired would take me 3 wks just to put on my climbing gear not worth it"*
>
> *"gotta pee but fat Ben blocks the tent door dad-gum him"*
>
> *"what the hell was I thinking"*

BREATHE... BREATHE IN THE AIR

Suck it up, buttercup.

To O_2 or not to O_2? That is the question. Some hardgals and hard-guys wouldn't dream of relying on supplemental oxygen. On the other side of Base Camp, novice climbers are sucking on that bottle like there's no tomorrow. There's also a hybrid strategy of climbing without oxygen until you reach the Death Zone, then strapping on the O-mask just before passing out. You'll know it's time when you need to pee but can't figure out how to unzip your fly.

Many superstars can climb at any height without oxygen aid. Ed Viesturs, for instance. But he also walks on water, so don't kid yourself that you can do it, too.

And for pity's sake, don't discard your empty bottle on the slope. Everest already has enough litter: frazzled ropes, fallen prayer flags, freeze-dried corpses. While you may not care about returning your empties for a 5-cent reward, desecrating the mountain drives up your karmic debt.

It's summit day! Yaay!

Finally, finally, *finally* all the pieces fall into place. You've reached Camp 4 with most of your body parts intact. Your group has whittled down to the grittiest, most cussedly stubborn climbers. The weather is perfect: 50 degrees below zero Fahrenheit with a wind chill of 170 below and whiteout snow conditions.

Here's how summit day typically plays out.

10 p.m. the night before Hoping to get a jump on other climbers, you peek out the tent flap for a weather check. To your dismay, other expeditions had the same idea; many are already climbing. You scramble to get your things together. You spill drinking water on your parka hood. You take a hit of bottled oxygen. You put your boots on the wrong feet. You stash a few sticks of beef jerky in your pocket and discover that you've been carrying your car keys all this way.

1 a.m. You've climbed 100 meters…

1:30 a.m.… in the wrong direction, following a band of rookies who left without their guide. Swine rookies! You turn around.

2 a.m. You pass Camp 4 again and follow the smarter climbers—who, incidentally, are going uphill.

2:03 a.m. Jagged icicles hang from the hood of your parka like the stalactites of Mammoth Cave.

2:15 a.m. You develop a nosebleed and wipe your nose on your parka sleeve.

3 a.m. Trudging uphill, you realize you've skipped breakfast, the most important meal of the day. You bite into the beef jerky. It shatters like glass.

4 a.m. The slope becomes steep and technical, requiring special tools. You ditched all your "technicals" at Camp 2 because they were too heavy.

4:01 a.m. A baseball-sized chunk of phlegm in your lungs leaves you gasping. You tell yourself you don't need the oxygen bottle yet.

4:02 a.m. After every step, you stop and take a dozen breaths. You tell yourself you can still make it without the O's.

4:03 a.m. The O_2 bottle is empty. You left the regulator valve open while scrambling to leave Camp 4.

4:04 a.m. Climbers tired of waiting single-file start pushing you uphill. You hallucinate about gliding effortlessly on a moving sidewalk in an airline terminal.

2 p.m. The motion stops. You blink and look around.

The other climbers have pushed you all the way to the summit. You made it. You did it. You should be ecstatic, but you're so exhausted you can't even summon an exclamation point.

You're wracked with a coughing spell. You cough up the baseball of phlegm and spit it out.

Climbing mates pull you in for a group photo. Later you'll recoil at your appearance: blood on your sleeve, phlegm on your chin, icicles hanging over your eyes like the grille of a monster pickup truck.

You remember to leave your deeply personal artifact, a tee shirt that says "I'm from Milwaukee, and that's not funny."

Just when we thought you couldn't get any dumber…

High-altitude climbing has the same aftereffect on your brain as electroshock therapy. Don't make any major decisions for a few months, like getting married or switching internet providers.

And don't be surprised if the folks back home aren't impressed by your Everest summit. Oh, Grandma will probably say, "I've always wanted to climb Mt. Everest," but that's about it. Maybe you can give a slide show at her assisted-living home. Some of the residents might even stay awake till the end.

CLIMB EVERY BIG-ASS MOUNTAIN

Abandon all hope, ye who enter here.

—DANTE'S INFERNO

Your first Everest expedition has changed you forever. For one thing, you're $60,000 poorer. And at cocktail parties, you may be slightly more interesting than, say, a stamp collector.

But once you've caught summit fever, civilization seems so dreary. Now you obsess over climbing lonelier peaks in a "purer" style, maybe just yourself and a loony-tune partner. You're about to become a real mountaineer.

Gear up, chump

When God created mountains, powerful outdoor-climbing lobbyists pushed for an infinite variety of snow, ice and rock. You've gotta be ready for every possible situation, right? So you buy crampons with foot-long points. Ropes from the thinnest spiderweb to a monster cord that could hold the *Queen Mary* at anchor. Every type of cam and nut ever invented.

Yet at some point you'll get stuck in a blinding snow squall, hanging on a 90-degree pitch that's covered with axle grease, 10W-40 and floor wax. And the single perfect piece of equipment that could save your life will be the one you didn't buy.

Oh well. Maybe your climbing partner brought that perfect piece of gear. If not, try praying. While that won't get you off the mountain alive, it might make you feel better about your next destination.

Other junk to bring

You'll need a good harness, not that lame rookie's belt from Tough Crap Warehouse. Look for a premium harness made of rich Corinthian leather with platinum fasteners.

For safely ascending fixed ropes, bring a pair of jumars: second cousins of a staple gun, they alternately slide along/grip a rope. Practice using them so that when your climbing mate falls into a crevasse, you'll know exactly what you're too freaked out to do. Also, a metal figure-eight descender for rappels lets you safely give up and go home.

Now's the time to upgrade your ice axe, Napoleon, and use your skills to:

- Δ balance on steep slopes.
- Δ chop steps or a tent platform in ice and hard-packed snow.
- Δ work out Camp 3 cabin fever by sword-fighting with your partner.

Choose whichever axe model is best adapted for a duel. Pretend you're Zorro: "Pointy end goes in the other man."

Your home away from home

How do outfitters design a 5-pound tent giving two climbers a safe and comfortable haven in a 90-mph blizzard? That's a trick question. It won't be "a safe and comfortable haven." Think more like "a porous, exasperating constant flapping in the wind, smaller than a breadbox, lighter than a Victoria's Secret thong little rag of a so-called shelter."

Lighten your load by carrying only one sleeping bag for the two of you. At night you unzip and pull it over yourselves while lying together in a spooning position—provided neither of you has eaten beans for supper.

You must also cram your mittens, water bottle, ice axe, canapes, and arrowhead collection into your sleeping bag to keep them from freezing overnight. These intrusions guarantee that you and your Zorro-poked partner will get no sleep and be super cranky in the morning.

Ice ain't nice

Your breath condenses as frost inside the tent, setting off a small blizzard as you move around and fluttering onto your face when you're trying to sleep.

Your fingers gradually turn numb. When at last there's a chance to thaw them, sensation returns with a sharp pain that veteran climbers call "the screaming barfies." Sometimes, wrapping your hands around a mug of hot tea is enough to start the thawing process. For severe frostbite, you might need to dunk your fingers in the mug, or even in the teapot. Whatever it takes, there's always tea involved.

What is it with tea and climbers, anyway? Read their memoirs: "We enjoyed our breakfast of tea and cardboard granola." "When I 'came to' after the avalanche, a Sherpa was pouring tea down my throat." "I had a quick supper of tea and tea." It's nothing but tea, tea, tea! Who cares if tea is the default beverage of the Himalayas? Couldn't you carry a hefty hot drink like Ovaltine or instant coffee? If it was good enough for the Greatest Generation, it should be good enough for you.

You don't really need those fingers, right?

Moving on to other foods and beverages…

What shall we eat? What shall we drink?

Your propane camp stove will melt snow for drinking water. At altitude, this chore takes three to four *hours*. To relieve the tedium, bring a nonstick griddle so you can flip some flapjacks at the same time. Yes, yes, the griddle weighs 25 pounds. But the entertainment value is worth it. What else are you gonna do all evening— reread *Crime and Punishment* for the nineteenth time?

You can't just gulp a handful of snow to stay hydrated. Melting snow in your mouth steals too much energy from your depleted carcass. And the higher you climb, the less appetizing ordinary food will seem. Junk food to the rescue! Potato chips, monstrous cookies, cheese puffs, donuts, tubs of margarine or lard, corn dogs, cotton candy—if these don't revive your appetite, you might as well pack up and head back to Muskogee.

Wherewithal shall we be clothed?

From the inside out, here's what you should wear.

1. A wicking layer of synthetic fabric. Avoid itchy wool, sweat-soaked cotton, or sackcloth made to repent for your sins.

2. Midlayer of wind fleece, created from the coats of wind sheep.

3. One-piece synthetic suit with drawstrings that narrow the hood into a tiny hole, making you look like an anteater.

4. Thick mittens with daycare-inspired "keeper strings" on your sleeves so you can't lose them.

5. Two pairs of wool/spandex socks. Boots with insulated inner parts and plastic outer shells. Insulated overboots of foam covered by Gore-Tex. Your feet now weigh 50 pounds. No wonder you're lurching around like Frankenstein's monster.

6. Under your hood: a heavy wool knit cap, and a wool balaclava that covers your neck and face all the way up to your eyes. Save that one in case you ever need to rob a bank.

7. Super-dark sunglasses that protect your eyes from ultraviolet radiation and make you look mysterious in that all-important summit photo.

Clean out the junk you've been carrying in your pockets for decades, like dead batteries, wadded Kleenex, an Oscar Mayer wiener whistle, and a tube of BBs. Then put it all back in, "just in case."

Keep your altimeter handy; knowing what altitude you've reached will confirm why you feel like death warmed over.

With every step you take, every move you make, be careful not to snag a front point of your crampons on your opposite leg. You might slide down into oblivion, giving your partner-enemy the last laugh. And don't wear your crampons inside the tent unless you're trying to create a ventilation mesh on the bottom panel.

So-so souvenirs

If you beat the odds and make it to the summit, you'll want to leave behind something that comes from the heart. Like your dog-eared copy of *No Shortcuts to the Top* with every single word high-lighted in yellow. Or the lucky carabiner you kissed at the summit of Everest, which then froze to your lips.

Never leave an item belonging to someone else. Imagine tell-ing your dad that his Purple Heart medal is safely stored at 8,000 meters in the Himalayas. There goes your inheritance.

Leave behind an heirloom for posterity.

PLAN NINE FOR UPPER SPACE

On this climb, unlike your Everest debut, there's no professional guide to tell you when to sleep, get up, eat, drink, pee, and put on your long johns. All of that is your responsibility on summit day.

1. The night before, set your old-fashioned metal alarm clock for 2 a.m.
2. Didn't bring the alarm clock? No worries. You're too nervous to sleep anyway.
3. At 2 a.m, curse the day you began this idiotic project.
4. Use unnecessary force to awaken your snoring partner.
5. Choke down an energy bar.
6. Stagger outside the tent and puke.
7. Argue with your partner over whether to bring the pancake griddle, because hey, wouldn't it look hilarious in the summit photo?

The final push

Trudge through the blizzard, icy air searing your lungs with every step. Fun, isn't it? Keep going uphill, as recommended by leading experts. Stop when there's nothing further to climb. (Check with your partner to make sure you're not hallucinating on a false summit.)

As you dimly realize you've reached the top, you might recall the old Peggy Lee tune "Is That All There Is?" Try to smile, despite your frozen jaw, while taking selfies with your partner.

Rummage in your pocket for the souvenir you meant to leave; watch your altimeter and old Kleenex get snatched away by the 90-mph wind. Then leave the summit sooner than you want to. Or hang around until dark and turn into a warning statue for future climbers.

Get back down in one piece

Apply everything you learned on the way up: If you're hungry enough, reconstituted split-pea soup is delicious. Never concede an inch of sleeping-bag space. Pee downwind.

Gravity is still your enemy. Don't be the show-off who unclips to glissade down a glacier.

You do have one advantage now that you're downclimbing: everything weighs less—even you. Exertion at altitude turned you into a skeleton, and a few frostbitten fingers and toes have snapped off. Best of all, you left that breakfast griddle at the high camp "so other climbers can use it." Yeah, right.

YOUR CLIMBING EXPEDITION FROM HELL

Climbing in the Himalayas is never cheap or easy. Like it or not, you're thrown together with several other serious climbers—usually strangers—who aim to summit the mountain at the same time.

The good news

Everybody has their own strengths. One guy knows somebody who knows somebody who can snag a coveted climbing permit in Nepal. Another lives off a trust fund with money to burn. The third guy is great with logistics; you'll never run out of freeze-dried chicken teriyaki. The fourth, who has previously climbed this mountain, knows the slightly-less-deadly routes. And the fifth, a woman, is a lightning-fast route-setting maniac.

The bad news

- Δ It's a multilingual group with no lingual in common.
- Δ Each climber has a radically different climbing plan: Leave 80-pound loads in random places on the mountain. Build three months' rest into the schedule. Go hard on all days ending in "y."
- Δ The loner seems to have a screw loose. Or maybe several screws.
- Δ One of the guys hates the gal, and the feeling is mutual.
- Δ One member is bossy, one is a born anarchist, and the others constantly shift allegiance like a herd of sheep.

Red flags

You know you're off to a bad start when: Someone added your name to the Base Camp memorial cairn for the mountain you're about to climb… All the green M&Ms mysteriously disappear from the mess tent jar… A voodoo doll bristling with stickpins hangs over the entrance to the toilet enclosure.

You need a strategy

Obviously, you'll need a strategy (or, as Bugs Bunny would say, a stra-TEE-jer-ree.) And although life's not all lovely thorns and singing vultures (as Morticia Addams would say), you should at least try to nip these problems in the bud (as Deputy Barney Fife would say). So get a move on.

Before leaving Base Camp

Use Google Translate to render these handy phrases in each teammate's language.

- Δ "That's the most asinine summit plan I've ever heard."
- Δ "Who dumped peanut butter in my sleeping bag?"
- Δ "It's my turn to lick the soup spoon."
- Δ "If you hum that song one more time, I'm gonna break your neck."
- Δ "Stop breathing my air."

When push comes to shove

- Δ Do unto others (push) before they can do unto you (shove).
- Δ Join the faction with the sharpest crampons.
- Δ Never stand between an enemy and an "objective hazard": cliff, crevasse, icefall—heck, just about anywhere on the mountain.
- Δ Carefully inspect your tent for trip wires before crawling in.

ARE YOU SMARTER THAN AN AVALANCHE?

Uh-oh. Too bad you left your avalanche beacon in Zurich.

You understand that mountains are living, brooding, cunning crea-tures. Yet you constantly cross their flanks—the mountain equiva-lent of a middle-finger salute. Fool! Daring them to retaliate!

Avalanches are the weapon of choice for murderous mountains. Let's assume you want to survive, even though many climbers at your level seem hell-bent on sleeping with the fishes. The more you know about that lethal white stuff, the more likely you'll live to middle-finger your way through another climb.

Oh, those wacky avalanches

In a *loose snow avalanche,* soft and powdery grains of snow sift into a huge mound that eventually collapses. You know: "Like sands through the hourglass, so are the Days of Our Lives." Or maybe you don't know, since you're always gone off on some dismal mountain with no time for the performing arts.

A *slab avalanche* occurs when a thick, frozen hunk of snow fractures and shears off: *Whumphfff.* You'll know it when you hear it. It's too late to get out of the way, but you'll be the smartest piece of debris in the avalanche field.

An avalanche rockets down the slope at up to 150 miles per hour. Sometimes it bottoms out in a valley and pushes its way up a neighboring mountain, catching other climbers *from behind.* Very tricksy, as Gollum would say.

An even more diabolical avalanche occurs when the forward edge of a glacier breaks: blocks of ice shear away like slices of Wisconsin cheese. The technical term for this process is *calving.* Yuck! Have you ever watched a livestock vet pull a baby calf out of its mother? I prefer the cheese simile, on toasted bread. Some of these sheared ice blocks are bigger than a car, a house or even an Amazon warehouse! Or Lambeau Field with a sellout crowd!! Try outrunning *that,* smartass climber!!!

An intriguing avalanche-in-waiting is the *hanging glacier,* created when reckless glacial ice-faces get stuck in a traffic jam. The notorious Bottleneck on K2 is a narrow couloir where climbers must pass beneath a hanging glacier. The hanging glacier's collapse can be really inconvenient if you're trying to stay alive.

An ice face on the lower edge of a hanging glacier is called a *serac,* which comes from a French word for a crumbly white cheese. Leave it to the French to associate a lethal element of nature with a tempting delicacy. "Would *monsieur* care for *le dessert? Un tranche de serac,* perhaps? A wafer-thin mint?"

An avalanche creates a windblast strong enough to kill nearby climbers and loud enough to be heard by stoned hippies all the way down in Bali. Avalanches can be triggered by warming temperatures, falling rocks, rising rocks, loud sneezes, negative thinking ("I don't like climbing anymore, waaahhh"), spicy food, kicking or scratching or swearing at the mountain, or reading a Dear John letter from your sweetheart back home.

Outsmarting an avalanche

Mountains will stop at nothing to smash you to smithereens. Here are some avalanche avoidance strategies, starting with the most drastic (you'll never try it) and ending with the easiest (which you'll probably never try, either).

△ Give up mountaineering. Enroll in the Federal Witness Protection Program for a new identity and a job at Cinnabon in Omaha, Nebraska.

△ Hire a sprint coach so you can dash to safety while the mountain chases your slower friends.

△ When native climbers conduct their puja ceremony asking for the mountain gods' blessing, pay attention instead of scrolling through your Tinder feed.

Desperate last-minute measures

Let's say you ignore all my brilliant suggestions and get caught in an avalanche. Immediately you should:

1. Grab hold of your ice axe.
2. If you haven't brought your ice axe, go back to Base Camp and get it.
3. Swing the axe into the ground as a brake.
4. Once the avalanche stops, pick your way through tons of snow and ice until you reach the surface. Allow a week or two for this process.
5. Remember the emergency transmitter beacon you left behind with other gear that was "just for sissies"? Next time, bring it along.

Don't bother reading online lists of "150 things to do in the middle of an avalanche." Like you're gonna remember any of them, right?... unless they're as egregious as this one: "Push away from yourself all machinery, equipment or heavy objects to avoid injury." So shove your John Deere tractor, Generac generator and barbells out of the way, and brace yourself.

"Climbing much better in Jamaica, mon."

Other avalanche strategies I stole from experts

Plan your trip.

△ Get a TripTik folder from AAA. Ask the travel agent to circle the unstable slopes with red pen.

△ Talk to climbers who recently descended your slope: "Was anybody in your group swept away by an avalanche?"

△ Have a safe alternate destination, like Jamaica.

Stay alert on mountains.

△ Watch for dangerous conditions: loose dry snow, wet slab snow, persistent or deep slab snow... so, basically: snow.

△ Avoid wishful thinking. That "freight train" you're hearing is highly unlikely on a 25-degree pitch at 9,000 feet above sea level.

△ Use a buddy system so someone else will be pulverized alongside you. Misery loves company.

Rally your group to rescue avalanche victims.

1. Determine how many climbers are missing. And are they really under the avalanche or still at Camp 2 playing poker?

2. Choose a leader to organize the search. The leader should be diligent, thorough, physically strong, mentally awake, and morally straight, with a merit badge in snowplowing.

3. Because the team must rescue victims within 10 to 15 minutes, it's imperative that every available person pitches in. If any survivors start panicking, slap them across the face and yell, "Snap out of it!"

Now you must personally resolve to Do The Right Thing. This could mean searching for clues and "deploying your probe in readiness," which sounds very GI Joe-like but simply means carrying a long metal pole. Or, Doing The Right Thing might mean getting the heck out of there before a copycat avalanche comes roaring down.

Take it easy with that probe, yo-yo.

Some guys have all the luck: rescuers

Let's say you decide to stick around. If the victim was carrying an avalanche transmitter beacon and the others have transceivers, stay out of their way while they begin a "coarse" search, narrowing it to a "fine" search and finally a "pinpoint" search. Then the leader will ask everyone to probe the snow for the buried chump. Handle your probe carefully to avoid goosing other rescuers.

Some guys have all the pain: victim

If a probe reaches a victim without fatally stabbing him, the leader hands out shovels. One person digs at the hot spot while others lean on their shovels like road construction workers. After freeing the victim, the team makes sure his mouth isn't filled with snow, granola or tea.

Then that poor old sod still isn't out of the woods, because moving him too quickly may send cold blood from extremities to the heart, causing cardiac arrest. Or the whole team, including an ignorant bystander like you, could be wiped out when the rescue

helicopter crash-lands at the scene. In the immortal words of Rose-
anne Rosannadanna: "It's always something."

So what have we learned?

- Δ Snow is a necessary evil. If the Big Bad 14 weren't covered
  with it, any wimp could reach the summit.
- Δ Snow is exciteable and unstable, like fans at a soccer match.
- Δ Snow has it in for you.

Some specialists regard avalanche dynamics and search techniques as a fascinating topic of study. These are the same guys
who can recite the value of "pi" to the 100th digit. Don't ever get
cornered by one.

And as for you? Just embrace the fact that climbing in avalanche
zones is a lottery. Better to be snuffed out in a few terrifying
seconds than to freeze solid slowly like a beef carcass at 24,000 feet.

EVEREST: A GUIDE FOR THE GUIDE

So you're saddled with a job you swore you'd never do: guiding a bunch of beginners on Everest. Yes, Everest, the Woodstock Festival of mountain peaks, with its blissed-out newbies, self-congratulatory vibes and mountains of trash. You are *so* over that scene—but you need the money.

The days of Everest guts and glory are long gone. For these amateurs, summiting the world's tallest peak is just another item on their bucket list, sandwiched between "floating in zero gravity in a SpaceX capsule" and "cheering the LA Lakers from a courtside seat next to Jack Nicholson."

Gilligan's Island at 29,000 feet

Your clients are a group of walking clichés, like characters in the old sitcom "Gilligan's Island." Even if you've never seen an episode, you'll recognize these personalities.

The Skipper got everybody into their predicament, botching a three-hour tour that stranded them on an uncharted island. In your case, this is the expedition director who hired you. He promised his clients ultimate bragging rights ("I climbed Everest!") at their next Uptown Leaders Smugfest.

Gilligan, perennial bumbler, strikes you as the guy most likely to plunge down a crevasse in the Khumbu Icefall. You'll be tempted to give him a shove. Don't do it. If you snuff the "little buddy" of The Skipper, he'll crush you in a headlock.

The Professor prepared for this trip by studying reams of data on high-altitude climbing. He's coolly curious to learn whether he'll lose any extremities to frostbite.

Ginger, the glamorous celebrity, posts selfies every five minutes to her millions of followers. She willingly paid for ten extra Sherpas to carry her gear, including a 70-pound bag of cosmetics.

Mary Ann is the all-American girl, cheerful and bright and friendly. Everyone loves her. If she dies, you're toast.

Thurston Howell III is all bluster and no bravado. At Everest's notorious traffic jams, he'll try to bribe his way to the front of the line.

Mrs. Thurston Howell III, fed up with her shallow lifestyle as a billionaire's wife with no first name, will remain in the Himalayas and become a Buddhist nun.

Everest Base Camp, from riches to rags

Climbers paid megabucks to join the expedition, and they expect top-level amenities. You, on the other hand, are used to self-deprivation. This comes into stark contrast at Everest Base Camp.

Food and beverages

Your climbing clients expect caviar, white truffles, Wagyu beef, oysters, and Moët & Chandon Imperial Vintage Champagne (1946). You prefer coffee grounds by the handful, melted snow, Aldi granola, plain oatmeal (cooked or uncooked, doesn't matter), and lentils.

Living quarters

Clients insist on multi-story tents, observation decks, home movie theaters with popcorn, and overnight shoeshine and dry-cleaning service. You want a lightweight bivy that's just strong enough to keep you from turning into a human popsicle.

Entertainment

Your clients prefer nightly shows by Cirque de Soleil, Elton John, Broadway touring companies, and the Rolling Stones. You're happy with a battery-lantern light and a tattered paperback edition of *Optimistic Nihilism.*

Communication
Your clients demand satellite phones as well as computers with the highest available speed. Your preferred level of contact: None.

Health and safety
Clients will produce mounds of litter during their six-week stay on Everest, yet they insist on occupying pristine areas when they arrive. You briefly consider pitching their tents over glacial fault lines.

It all boils down to the love/hate relationship you have with your clients. They love you. You hate them, yet you musn't let it show. Besides, you do like them a little, since the paycheck for this gig helps feed your mountaineering addiction.

"Don't bother me. I'm monk-ing."

Even hypochondriacs get sick sometimes

From the moment first-timers arrive at Base Camp, they start worrying about their health. They keep on worrying even after the expedition's doctor assures them they're fine. So you, the hardened climber, must do a little hand-holding—which is a bit like asking a cloistered monk to give a Ted Talk.

To make this easier, use these simple answers to typical complaints.

Δ Lung-shredding cough. "Lungs are resilient. I'm doing fine with just the 5% of tissue that's left."

Δ Dysentery. "Drink this gallon of Gatorade and call me in the morning."

Δ Blinding headache. "Ice usually helps. Go outside and press your forehead on the ground."

Δ Nausea, loss of appetite. "Here's a coupon for a half-price meal plan on your next expedition."

Δ Altitude sickness. "Maybe you're just not cut out for this climbing thing."

Once the Everest trip is over, take the money and run to a real change of pace: K2.

"HEY, ASKOLE!"

The approach to mighty K2, the world's second-highest mountain, isn't dangerous. But don't let that put you off. It's a world-class dirt scene.

The experience begins when your plane lands in Skardu, Pakistan, gateway to the 8,000-ers of the Karakoram mountain range. Though the valley is beautiful, notice how the place-names— Karakorams, K2, Skardu, Pakistan—are stuffed with a's and k's... a subtle foretaste of the hacking cough that soon will strangle your airways. *Akk, akk, aaakkk.*

To get from Skardu to the trailhead, you must pay for a jeep ride. You know jeeps are no-frills, right? Hard seats and no window glass, or standing-room-only in the truck bed. It seems like a grand adventure: fresh air, scenery, getting it on like a local.

Off you go, then.

The greater Skardu metro area.

Things get down and dirty as soon as you leave Skardu. What happened to all those beautiful lakes, forests, flowers? What happened to everything but dirt and rocks? Nobody told you that Skardu is zoned for beauty, while all the rest is zoned for dirt. And the driver makes sure you get your full 85-kilometers' worth of it. It reminds you of going to church on Ash Wednesday: "Remember that you are dust, and to dust you shall return."

The road climbs steadily. The dirt walls close in. *Akk aakkk aaaakkkk.* Your lungs don't like this.

Most climbers regard the hike to the Baltoro Glacier and K2's Base Camp as a necessary evil. It begins when your driver dumps you off in the village of Askole. Yes, Askole. The Askole of the World is the only place you can holler "Hey, Askole!" at total strangers and not get beat up.

In dust we trust

Surprisingly, there is room for improvement in Askole. A mud hut would be considered luxury housing, because it takes water to make mud. What's more, this place had tiny, tiny, *tiny* houses before tiny houses became a thing. Askole's Tourism Bureau could kick-start the urban renewal by recruiting a classy coffee shop and a B&B. "The Inn at Askole" has a nice ring to it. Then throw in a craft brewery and a five-star bistro.

But that's the last thing *you* would want. Askole is the final human settlement before the slog to the Karakorams, and humble though it is, you can't wait to leave behind the annoying buzz of humanity.

Ed Viesturs gets this. He calls the wilderness trek from Askole to K2 an "approach march" that's "wild, harsh, and dusty." Calling this region *dusty* is like saying the Sun is hot. The march is nothing but dust, stones, rocks, and more dust. Betcha can't wait to get back there for another go at Killer K2.

GUYS AND GALS

And now for some gratuitously sexist advice…

Hey, guys!

Here's a couple words of advice about partners and children: Don't have them. Oh, heck, that was three words. Might as well say more.

You never see it coming. One minute you meet someone charming. The next minute you're a couple of penguins mated for life, with a flock of little penguins waddling and squawking and needing an endless supply of little penguin-y things.

Life is messy. It's way messier when one of you has climbmania. No doubt you fit Joe Simpson's profile: "I was a penniless, narrow-minded, anarchic, abrasive and ambitious mountaineer." Not exactly a candidate for Best Dad on the Block.

The Death Zone isn't just a peak above 26K; it's also where your marriage exists when you're away from home 11.5 months of the year. You may be vaguely aware of all the chores you've dodged: meals, laundry, paying the bills, power-washing the kids' playroom and the kids, scooping & scraping pet poop indoors and out.

But let's be fair. Your loved ones never consider the great stuff you're missing on the home front. Like the pride of being told during a parent-teacher conference that your son likes eating Play-Doh. The hilarity of witnessing your dog skid into the bar cart and smashing every last liquor bottle, including that rare barrel-aged Scotch from your honeymoon. The intimacy of your wife's reminder that you're overdue for a colonoscopy.

Homesick in the Death Zone

Most of all, family ties are a huge distraction. Being so far apart gives every home-related memory a rosy glow. Bundled in your sleeping bag just before the summit push, you kiss a laminated snapshot of your wife, kids and pets. You ache to see them again. You worry that your life insurance policy doesn't cover falls over 10,000 feet. Distraction, distraction.

Finally you come home. A wave of tenderness warms your heart. You give everybody a big hug. Ten minutes later you're entrenched in your home office, planning the next big climb. The kids pound on the door. Your wife yells that you promised to fix the dishwasher. The cat wraps around your neck like a fur stole, its claws embedded in your windpipe.

Work/life balance? There isn't any. To quote Kurt Russell in "Tombstone," "That's the damnable misery of it."

If you can't beat 'em, bring 'em along

Who says family togetherness requires staying home? Why don't these clingy people come along with you for a change? Get your kids and insignificant other involved in your climbs. That'll learn 'em. Your wife can carry 50-pound loads to Base Camp. Your kids can ride on the backs of Sherpas.

The Base Camp cooking crew would be delighted to have The Missus lend a hand, especially if she brings along your thoughtful Christmas gift-book, *Fifty Fabulous Lentil Casseroles*. The kids can peel potatoes, tote water, and wash the Sherpas' feet in gratitude for their piggyback rides.

Frequently remind your family members how lucky they are for this experience. Where else could they wake up in such rarefied air with a splitting altitude headache? Or gaze at the fierce mountain summit where you'll soon be risking your neck? They'll come to appreciate everyday luxuries back home: Drinking water that's not downstream from a latrine. No goraks—giant Himalayan ravens—pecking away at dead rodents. Mattresses and box springs instead of threadbare blankets spread over rocks. Freedom from tuberculosis, dysentery, typhoid and chronic obstructive pulmonary disease.

Hey, gals!

In the bad old days, self-appointed experts told women that climbing would make their ovaries fall out. But the truth is, women deliberately stayed on the sidelines so they could watch men learn by trial and error, climbing the Matterhorn in woolen kilts and using ropes made of chicory root fiber.

"Ye need a tarrtan furr climbin', that's furr shurr."

Today, women have claimed their rightful place, proving that they can fall off a mountain as well as any man. In fact, multiple women are among the world's best rock climbers because of their greater flexibility and pain tolerance. (To make a mother laugh, ask how her husband would cope with labor pains.)

Rock climbing is similar to tree climbing, which women have evolved to perfection. When sabre-tooth tigers charged the clan, women carried rocks up trees and waited until the beasts came within striking distance. Men charged toward the tigers with two-foot spears.

The dark side

Some women athletes become obsessed with calories and weight loss, further complicated by the typical climber's raging sweet tooth. High-energy drinks, "protein" (candy) bars and goopy gels are 99% sugar, sending you higher than the summit.

Elite women climbers have broken the glass ceiling, the icefall ceiling and the serac ceiling on their way to the top. Sadly, some paid the ultimate price. Gravity is an equal-opportunity destroyer.

Here's a real "tough mudder": Annapurna

In 1978, an all-female climbing team hoping to make history on Annapurna slogged through leeches, a breakdown in the tampon supply chain, and a near-fatal level of bruised egos and hurt feelings. And that was just the trek to Base Camp.

"The leeches are quite intelligent," expedition leader Arlene Blum wrote in *Annapurna: A Woman's Place*. Those leeches knew better than to "spend eighty thousand dollars and risk our lives to try to stand on top of Annapurna." The leeches feasted on climbers' exposed skin, and "squat quickly if you have to squat" became their toilet tactic.

Expedition friction

As climbers carried supplies up the mountain, personalities clashed. Matters came to a head over a six-hour breakfast as the oatmeal congealed. Team members squabbled about the group's structure. Should it be a democracy? Benevolent dictatorship? "Lord of the Flies" summer camp? Finally one climber said, "Let's quit blabbing. This psychological crap is a waste of time." The group voted by secret ballot. Final tally: Quit Blabbing 10, Psychological Crap 3.

Pulling together as a team once again, the climbers would eventually make the first American ascent of the 10th highest mountain in the world, which is also considered one of the most challenging.

On its first ascent, back in 1950, Maurice Herzog's team spent weeks simply finding Annapurna. Officially known as Annapurna I (Main), it is surrounded by other peaks named Annapurna I Central, Annapurna I East, Annapurna II, Annapurna III, Annapurna IV, Annapurna South, and Annapurna Fang. I am not making any of this up. If I were, I'd say the entire region was surrounded by a barbed wire fence, and Herzog's expedition had to send a runner back to France for a wire cutter.

Back to the futile

The higher the '78 women's team climbed and the harder they worked, the bonier they became. "Our bosoms were vanishing," Blum wrote. Poachers were probably involved. In Nepal there's a high demand for big American breasts.

As with any big-mountain climb, there were moments of danger and suspense. On one treacherous slope at 20,000 feet, the lead climber was stymied by a snow gully until finally she secured a deadman protective piece.

Who names this stuff? A *deadman* is just a hunk of metal masquerading as Swiss cheese. But somebody, somewhere thought it would be funny if customers walked into an outdoor-gear store asking for a "dead man." For all we know, the store might have a bunch of actual dead men stacked like cordwood in the back room: former salespeople who ditched work for a quickie climb that turned out to be their last. Notice that there's no corresponding "deadwoman" metal piece. That's a sex-discrimination class action lawsuit waiting to happen.

And what's up with the term *crampons,* which sounds like shorthand for cramps + tampons? Not something any woman would covet.

FIRST SUMMITS: GRAB YOURS NOW

Admit it. You hunger and thirst for a first: the first summit of a significant peak that'll make you a superstar in the mountaineering crowd. But all the good summits have been taken by individuals and teams of every nation; climbers who have overcome every sort of physical handicap; and climbers who go without ropes, tools or common sense.

Never fear. That lack of common sense also resides in your DNA. You can tap into it just by thinking way, way, *way* outside the box.

Dog breath keeps you warm at Camp 3.

First summits of all fourteen 8,000-ers are still available in the
following categories.

Δ First summit with your service dog, service miniature horse,
   comfort parakeet, emotional support sandhill crane, or
   service goldfish.

Δ First summit wearing only a Speedo.

Δ First summit while holding your breath.

Δ First summit carrying the Olympic torch.

Or better yet, do them all at once! This summit strategy will require
tremendous mental toughness. Holding your breath and freezing
your Speedo-clad butt at Base Camp, trying to keep the Olympic torch from sputtering out, straining to control your gung-ho
canine—even you, the mountain maniac, might wonder: *Is this
a good idea?* Getting off on the right foot is vital, even if you've
already lost most of your right foot to frostbite.

Having lots of money on the line will shore up your willpower. The
trouble is, your usual sponsors won't get behind this crazy stunt.
Well, screw them! You can line up new sponsors who'll love your
focused approach: Pentland Brands for the Speedo… Best Friends
Animal Society for your rescued dog… the International Olympic
Committee for the torch—hey, they might even make this an offi-
cial sport of the Winter Olympics.

What have you got to lose, other than your professional reputa-
tion, your pride, and your frozen butt cheeks? Go for it, I say!

PRACTICAL JOKES AT 24,000 FEET

After your record-setting solo trek, you'll probably wish for the relative ease of climbing alongside other elite hardasses. Admittedly, that didn't end well last time. The woman climber did jail time for aggravated assault, and the Australian went on all the talk shows with sensational stories of cannibalism (when really, all you did was bite his ear).

But don't give up so easily. People get a little testy when every labored breath could be their last. The following tips will lighten the mood of your next climbing party. Just make sure the jailbird and the Aussie don't get invited.

During the climb: Squeeze a fart cushion inside your snowpants so it burps with every step… Complain of snow blindness, then pull off your sunglasses to reveal a pair of googly eyes… Tape a "Kick me" sign on the back of someone's parka… At the summit, hand out congratulatory exploding cigars.

In the tent: Bring a klaxon horn for the 2 a.m. wakeup call on summit day… Sneak a spring-loaded toy snake into the rations box… Slip a pair of Groucho glasses on someone when they're sleeping… Open the tent flap, reach out, and pull in "tonight's dinner": a rubber chicken.

On the downclimb: Shout "Avalanche!!!" as you glissade past them.

Perennially witty travel remarks: "Are we there yet?" and/or "Are we having fun yet?"… "There's Wall Drugs billboard number 1 (25, 75, 100, etc.)."… "Let's play 'I see something white.'"

Everybody sing! "Ninety-nine bottles of beer on the wall"… "It's a beautiful day in the neighborhood"… "Hi ho, hi ho, it's off to work we go" *(whistle)*… "There's a big yellow thing on a flatbed trailer / wonder what that thing's for"… "Super-cali-fragil-istic-expi-ali-do-cious"… "It's a small world after all."

PART III½
ROCKHEADS

Habitat: *Sheer rock faces*
Skill level: *You rock.*

Rock-wall climbing doesn't have blizzards and avalanches, but don't worry—it's just as dangerous and foolhardy as mountaineering.

BIG-WALL AID CLIMBING: GO BIG OR GO HOME

Big-wall routes are physically tough and mentally intimidating. It takes days to climb them—or months, or even decades if you don't know what you're doing.

You'll sleep on a portaledge, which you anchor into the rock after finishing each day's pitch. It's like being a window washer on a skyscraper, except you don't get paid and you don't go home at night.

Imagine your childhood treehouse without sides, a sturdy roof, or the friendly tree, and so narrow that you and your climbing buddy must sleep with one's head next to the other's feet. How fun.

"Oops, there goes our water jug."

While mountain climbing allows everybody and his derelict brother on the team, most rock-wall climbing is limited to just the leader and the belayer.

A rock climb usually involves just two people because…
   1. I don't know.

Maybe because you'll be lucky to find even one person willing to go with you. Traditional mountain climbs often begin on gradual slopes that look easy, whereas rock climbing looks dangerous from the get-go. Also, rock climbing carries risks like the "zipper effect" that instantly pluck careless climbers off the wall. Experienced climbers who turn down your invitation see a zipper in your future.

Assuming you're the leader, you can…

   Δ lead the route. So far, so good.
   Δ place protection as you go.
   Δ set up each belay station.
   Δ call the whole thing off if you get scared, hungry or bored.

Your belayer can…

   Δ argue over your decision to bail, because she/he isn't scared, hungry or bored.
   Δ follow you up the wall while "cleaning" protection pieces, especially if they're covered with bird droppings.
   Δ feed out rope, anticipating your need for tension or slack.
   Δ update you on rope status—ideally, sometime before you're literally at the end of your rope.

Be honest about your ability to lead a difficult climb. If you have trouble climbing cracks, avoid a crack-infested route. Just don't tell your friend you have a "crack problem" or they might schedule an intervention. If you're afraid of heights, pop a Xanax before you leave the ground.

A route already protected by bolts can be a good place to practice leading. Your belayer partner doesn't need to know ahead of time that you're practicing. She'll figure it out soon enough.

Let's start getting started

As you're approaching the rock face, look upward at your intended route. Watch for deep chimneys where parrots and macaws might be lurking. Look for bushes partway up the rock wall where you can rest and take a leak. Pay special attention to spray-painted climbing graffiti like *This route sucks.*

Then develop a plan for leading the pitch.

△ Can you and your belayer call out to each other? If not, will you use smoke signals? Radios? (If you answer "How can we use radios if you didn't tell us to bring any?" you need to remember that I'm not your mother.)

△ If you fall, how will this affect the belay? (If you answer "I'm not sure," play it safe by sinking a protective piece every six inches.)

△ How will you minimize the likelihood of a zipper-effect fall? (If you answer "I don't know, 'cause you still haven't explained the zipper effect," thank you for staying awake.)

Win this one for the zipper

The zipper effect happens when you place protection in an idiotic pattern that leaves the rope zigzagging across the rock. If you fall, the protective chocks pop out one by one, starting at the top, like a zipper sliding open. It's quite impressive, and onlookers will give you a big round of applause—which you might be too dead to appreciate.

Boring technical stuff

Big-wall aid climbing uses protective pieces to "aid" in resisting gravity. If you've been lusting after gear like the Camalot, offset Aliens, micronuts, the Yates Screamer, and the Petzl Grigri—instead of things normal people lust after—you've found your niche.

Then there's malleable heads: pliable tools that can be hammered into cracks without breaking. You can *pound* the head, *paste* the

head and *pin* the head. It's a great way to work out your pent-up
anger over lying awake last night on the portaledge while your
restless sleeping partner kept kicking your face.

You can't hang all those pieces willy-nilly on your climbing
harness, belt or jock strap. Well, actually you can, though you'll
regret it later when your shoulder is stuck in a narrow crack
and the next piece you need is on the buried side of your waist.
Arrange the pieces however you like, either alphabetically, or in
the order you bought them, or with the familiar ones close at hand
and the ones you don't know how to use at the far end.

With hundreds of tools hanging around your waist, you'll resemble
a telephone lineman. Let the old saying "Better to have and not
need than to need and not have" be your guide, and keep adding
tools until the belts and your pants are puddled around your
ankles.

For the long haul
On a multi-day climb you'll cram tons of junk into a nylon haul
bag and hoist it up the wall with ropes, hitches and anchors. Since
you're no longer carrying everything on your back, bring all your
favorite heavyweights: dumbbells, beer kegs, vintage Led Zeppe-
lin heavy metal albums. Keep in mind that the bag will trigger
rockfalls; make sure you're leading every pitch.

Can you stash all this crap in YOUR haul bag?

Daredevil moves

You've foolishly climbed off-route. Now a "2001: A Space Odyssey" monolith looms between you and safe ground. Try a *tension traverse:* moving horizontally with a tight rope. The first time you try this, every cell in your brain will scream "Nooo!" But after you've done it a few times… every cell in your brain still screams "Nooo!" because your brain knows that a suicidal stunt doesn't improve with practice.

With the *Tyrolean traverse,* your rope becomes a makeshift zipline for crossing a river or moving between a wall and a detached pinnacle. The big difference: a conventional zipline is a fun ride that's been safely set up for tourists, while the Tyrolean traverse must be set up by you-know-whoohoo, with plenty of potential boo-boos, like getting stuck halfway across.

Take special precautions when *climbing an overhang*. Use runners (extension pieces, not athletes) to hold the rope beyond the rock edge. This helps avoid sawing the rope in two, which is considered a poor outcome. When traversing a ledge, place protection all along the move to avoid launching your partner into an *unintentional pendulum*—another dramatic crowd-pleaser that's not as much fun as it looks.

Don't use double- or twin-rope techniques until you have a few decades of experience. And by then you'll be so beat up that you won't want to climb at all.

OH SOLO YOU-OH

Mind games

Now that you're thoroughly sick of big-wall lead climbing, it's time to go solo. Ditch your partner. Ditch most of your gear. Ditch your rational mind, if you haven't already.

Solo climbing might be the most nerve-wracking challenge you've faced since you flunked your driver's license test. Three times. At least trying out for a license didn't carry the risk of a fatal fall. No wonder you're scared shiftless.

Become "one" with the wall

Let's get all Zen about this. The wall wants you to succeed. Yes, that's hard to believe when the wall is raining dozens of rocks on your head or shearing off holds that looked like a sure thing. It's just that the wall knows you're making the wrong moves; those rocks and sheared flakes are nudges in the right direction.

Stop. Tune in. Can you feel the wall's heartbeat? Can you hear it breathing? Of course not—that's ridiculous. Forget I said it. But when the wall seems to make things hard on purpose, look around for alternate moves. Remember the Talking Heads line: "There's a million ways to get things done." Although your arms will be pumped to the failing point before you try the remaining 999,994 ways, it's good to start with a nice round number.

Embrace your inner Ronald McDonald

Have fun on the route! You're not getting a root canal. You *wanted* to do this, remember?

Pretend you're a chimpanzee just hangin' out. Or a house fly inching across a hunk of peanut brittle. Or King Kong, standing atop the Empire State Building and pounding his chest. Just be sure to double-check the connections on your harness before trying any of these incredibly fun games.

Chimps just wanna have fun.

Get some perspective

Climbers naturally zone in on the rock right in front of them. Yet when you're stuck, it pays to try another perspective. Imagine looking down at your puny self from the top of the cliff. Or standing at ground level, watching your own butt. Or as a single cell in your colon, wondering what it ever did to deserve this fate.

Then return to your current point of view. Feel any different? At the very least, you should feel happy to be outside your colon. Take it from there.

Review your "highlights reel"

For an emotional boost, review some of your recent achievements…

…at anything, not just climbing…

…this may take a while…

OK, start really small, like when you remembered to buy the right brand of kitty litter so your mom's finicky cat wouldn't start pooping all over the house again. Or how you changed into a clean t-shirt for your mandatory follow-up visit to the unemployment office.

Now tell yourself: *If I can do that, I can certainly climb this wall, which is several grades of technical difficulty above my previous climbs.* That's the theory, anyway.

Hang in there

I won't bore you with famous quotes about perseverence. You've certainly heard and ignored them all. But think of it this way: being the most cussedly stubborn S.O.B. often makes the difference between the winner and the also-rans. Decide that you won't quit, no matter what.

True, this attitude can also be the difference between the safe down-climber and the headstrong idiot who gets carted away in a basket hanging from a helicopter. But which one makes the local six-o'clock newscast, right?

Lost in space

Elite climbers are superbly in tune with their body's subtle cues to reposition their stance or adjust a finger hold. Getting to this level of awareness takes deliberate practice. If you're not listening to subtle cues, you'll get more and more out of whack until your body sends an absolutely unsubtle cue like "You're gonna fall, nimrod!"

On the other hand, you must block out unhelpful cues:

- Δ *Growling stomach:* "It's been 2 hours since your last granola bar."
- Δ *Itchy eyes:* "Pleeaase rub me."
- Δ *Lower intestine:* "Shoulda brought the poop tube."

Do some soul-searching to figure out why you get sewing-machine leg even before you leave the ground, or why you're compelled to check every 30 seconds that the fly of your shorts is still zipped. Ask yourself: *Am I overly concerned about how I look to other people?* (Yes.) *Do I have what it takes for a Class 1 climb?* (No.) *Is my problem physical, emotional, or technical?* (Yes, yes, and yes.)

Now that you've identified your laundry list of problems, it may be tempting to give up. And you probably should. Hey, I'm gonna be a Debby Downer here: the odds that you'll master solo climbing are about the same as a rhinocerous who wants to do needlework.

Practice makes barely acceptable

Your one chance might be to get angry and try to prove me wrong. Go ahead, I can take it. Maybe you'll practice the same route over and over, paying attention to what doesn't work and trying other moves instead. With each attempt you'll use your new moves and discover more of them. That's what you should have been doing all along. It actually works. Imagine that.

FREE CLIMBING: PLAYING CHICKEN WITH THE ROCK WALL

Free climbing involves using only your own body for upward prog-ress. A rope and minimal protection are there to save you in case of a fall—but only if you haven't messed up your pro, numbskull.

Rock star Lynn Hill

In 1993, American climber Lynn Hill, along with Brooke Sandahl, became the first person ever to free-climb the Nose route on Yosemite's El Capitan. The next year she became the first person to free climb the entire route in a single 24-hour period. By compari-son, the climb usually took at least four days of aid climbing.

Fate seems to have blessed Lynn with the perfect combination of strength, flexibility and rock-smarts. Maybe that's no coincidence: According to the theory of "nominative determinism," people gravitate toward careers that reflect their names. Thus, Lynn *Hill* climbed to the upper reaches of the sport.

Lynn is not only greatly talented but also friendly and humble. Just admit that you're burning with envy. Long ago you missed the opportunity to change your name to Norman Rockwall, and you've been playing catch-up ever since.

Yes, then there's you

So there you are, poised on a microscopic flake, 50 feet above your last piece of cheap, lame protection. You took a risk that won't end well. As every finger and toe starts slipping, you've got, at best, 10 seconds to make your move.

Lynn Hill's uncanny flexibility would lead her out of this quandary. But you're not Lynn. Tommy Caldwell (coming up next) would breeze through the challenge as well. You're not Tommy, either.

I have no smartass tips for you. Prepare to meet your Maker. Or, for you nihilists out there, prepare to become null and void.

"Hail Mary, full of grace..."

Rock star Tommy Caldwell

Tommy, along with Kevin Jorgeson, made the first free climb of the Dawn Wall on Yosemite's El Capitan in 2015. Some considered this 19-day ascent to be the hardest successful free climb ever.

Mike Caldwell immersed his son Tommy in rock climbing and mountaineering from an early age with an intensity Tommy calls "pure genius." While always staying within safe limits, Mike led 6-year-old Tommy and his 8-year-old sister Sandy to the top of Devil's Tower in Wyoming. At age 12, Tommy followed Mike up nearly 2,000 vertical feet of granite on the Diamond route of Longs Peak in Colorado.

If you chose your parents unwisely and wasted your formative years being car-pooled to soccer matches and cheer competitions, you're already light-years behind Tommy. With a focused campaign of extreme diligence, you might catch up to Tommy's preteen level by the time you're eligible for Social Security.

FREE SOLO: ROCK-WALL RUSSIAN ROULETTE

Rock star Alex Honnold

On June 3, 2017, in less than four hours, Alex made the first free solo climb of El Capitan—Yosemite's perilous 3,000-foot granite wall—without ropes, protective gear, or any assistance from a partner. *National Geographic* called this "the greatest feat of pure rock climbing in the history of the sport."

Whereas the "death zone" in mountaineering occurs at 8,000 meters (26,000 feet), in free climbing it's just 100 feet. If you're any higher than that, a fall would kill you. See how efficient free climbing can be?

Like Lynn Hill and Tommy Caldwell, Alex is friendly, likeable, and humble. If you saw him on the street, you'd never guess that he's a knight in the Royal Order of the Gecko.

Alex began solo climbing because he was too shy to ask strangers if he could rope up with them. Soon he discovered that "if I had any particular gift, it was a mental one—the ability to keep it together in what might otherwise have been a stressful situation."

For major climbs, Alex rehearsed his sequence of moves on top-rope. He also spent days just sitting and visualizing every move on the route. The actual climb was simply an execution of his plan.

In one particularly tough freeclimbing situation, Alex's fingers and toes barely touched the wall, yet he was certain he wouldn't fall—and that certainty kept him from falling. This transcendent moment occurred in April 2008 as he made the first-ever free climb of Moonlight Buttress in Zion. When insiders learned of his achievement, Alex, age 22, became an overnight sensation. And he's been sensational ever since.

Don't even think about it
In case you're daydreaming of pulling off an El Cap free solo, I'll set you straight. If you have enough spare time to read this goofy book, you're not Alex Honnold, you never will be, and attempting this climb with anything less than an exalted state of Honnoldness would be a Big Mistake.

Still dead set on the idea (with emphasis on the "dead")? Read Part IV and plan accordingly, meatball.

Other famous daredevils
If somehow you find success as a free soloist, you're in good company. The following men have established a direct correlation between testosterone and insanity.

Nik Wallenda walked a 2-inch wire over Niagara Falls, crossing 1,800 feet from the U.S. side to Canada. At the Canadian border, his stunt unexpectedly became a round trip because he'd forgotten his passport.

Philippe Petit, a French high-wire artist, walked a tightrope strung between the Empire State Building in New York and the Sears Tower in Chicago in just two weeks.

Evel Knievel: This famed motorcyclist cleared the fountain at Caesar's Palace in Las Vegas, as well as 14 Greyhound buses in Cincinnati, Ohio. Knievel also holds the Guinness world record for 433 fractures, the most broken bones in a lifetime. His un-cremated remains reside in a two-ounce pillbox at Forest Lawn Hollywood Hills.

Larry Walters attached 45 helium balloons to his patio chair, rose to 16,000 feet, and landed in high-voltage power lines. Afterward he told reporters, "I had this dream for 20 years, and if I hadn't done it,

I think I would have ended up in the funny farm." Which is probably where he ended up anyway.

Harry Houdini was placed inside a washing machine with shackles
on his arms and legs. Thirty minutes later, he emerged with a clean
load of whites.

Harry Houdini in mid-trick.

Alain Robert, the "French Spider-Man," has climbed more than 100
skyscrapers and monuments with his bare hands. He says he plans
to keep climbing until his body tells him to stop (since his mind
apparently has no say in the matter).

Luciano Pavarotti once performed the tenor aria "Ah mes ami"
beneath a Dale Chihuly chandelier, hitting all nine high C's until
every piece of glass had shattered around him.

OH, THE PLACES YOU WON'T GO

Places with weird faces

Rock 'n roll bands have weird names. Lunatics at Burning Man have weirder names. But nothing comes close to weird names assigned to difficult rock faces. Usually they're named by the first climber(s) who summit them. No wonder they're weird.

As a hard-man or -woman, you may think you've heard them all—so you'll want to test yourself on these. After all, mental hardship is 99% of your life. (The other 1% is getting to & from the hardship.)

Two of these groups are real names. The other two are fake. Guess which is which.

Group 1: Acrophobics Anonymous, There Goes the Neighbor-hood, Asshole from El Paso, Timeless Christian Values, Sphincter Quits, Unemployed Black Astronaut, Debby Does CPR

Group 2: The Brainy Bunch, Wash Your Cat, Dejected Sand Flea, Thin Like a Pencil, Who Stole the Kishka, Another Day's Useless Energy Spent

Group 3: A Good Day to Die, Sump Pump, The Comfy Chair, Dizzy Spell, Citizen's Arrest, Go in Piss

Group 4: The Cat's Ears, Shipton Spire, Godzilla, Hairstyles and Atti-tudes, The Mystery Phallus

ANSWERS

Groups 2 and 3 are fake. Groups 1 and 4 are real—assuming you can trust an obscure online forum, as I did.

PART IV
FREE-FALLIN': DEAD

Habitat: six feet under… scattered to the wind in the Black Canyon of the Gunnison… or sitting on a fireplace mantel until the cat upsets the urn, which shatters on the floor and prompts Spouse to mutter, "One last descent. How appropriate."

Skill level: Legendary

You're hard-rocking the **rockhead** phase when:

△ You can't remember the last time you had toenails.

△ You get junk mail from funeral pre-planning services offering an Early Bird Special.

△ On rare visits home, you spend every waking hour hanging by your fingertips in the kitchen doorway.

△ Your spouse files for divorce on the grounds of alienation of affection, with your chalk bag as Exhibit A.

And you're beyond **mountaineering mania** when:

△ Your ears no longer pop at high elevations, because your eardrums are trashed.

△ With a rare free day in your calendar, you fly home to watch your son's T-ball game, only to learn that he just graduated from college.

△ Due to extensive frostbite damage, you're frequently mistaken for Alice Cooper.

△ Sherpas in Kathmandu build a community center out of your discarded oxygen tanks.

Δ   On a risk-taking scale, where 1 is a tax accountant and 10 is a
    kamikaze pilot, you're rated 13.

Wake up, hardass.
You're plunging down the couloir of life without an ice axe—
        headed straight toward
            annihilation…

Here's your final climbing partner.

QUOTES THAT WILL INSPIRE YOU... TO QUIT

"What the hell—climbing is dangerous."
—GREG CHILD

"Annapurna started to become not a mountain but a being that wants to kill you. I had the feeling of an animal in front of a hunter. He doesn't want to kill you at once; he wants to torture you first."
—JEAN-CHRISTOPHE LAFAILLE

"Throughout the whole descent, which took two and a half days, there were three of us: Norbert, myself, and fear."… "Here was a place that ought to be reserved only for those who are tired of life."
—ERHARD LORETAN, DOWNCLIMBING WITH NORBERT JOOSE ON ANNAPURNA'S DUTCH RIB

"The mountain was lit harshly by the sun, and in the shade it was cold blue. K2 looked like a monster."… "You can't accurately calculate all the odds; maybe God is unhappy with you one day."
—ANATOLI BOUKREEV

"I had never seen a mountain sight so numbing, so haunted with impossibility and danger."
—DAVID ROBERTS, CLIMBING THE REMOTE MOUNTAIN DEBORAH IN ALASKA'S HAYES RANGE

Fall Off the Mountain

(Tune: "Climb Every Mountain" from "The Sound of Music")

Fall off the mountain, drag down your team
You're so high in space that no one hears you scream
Though Search & Rescue looks high and low
They will never find you, buried in the snow

The snow that you hoped you could always outlive
Till an avalanche came, crushing you through a sieve

Fall off the mountain, wave life goodbye
They'll write on your tombstone: "Dumbass way to die!"

FIFTEEN WAYS TO LEAVE YOUR LIFETIME

Rockheads

Crux: The part of the route most likely to kill you.

Dyno move: Leaping to what should be your next hold. This often reveals itself—mid-leap—as the crux (see above).

Crack: A defect in your brain that compels you to attempt suicidal climbs.

Smear: Pushing off the wall with the sole of your climbing shoe. Also: what remains of you at the base of the climb if you screw up this move.

Approach: Walking to the base of a climb; nearly all fatal climbs begin with an approach.

Mountain morons

Frostbite: The mountain's oddball way of saying "I love you, you're perfect, now freeze."

Glissade: Deliberately sliding down a steep, icy slope. Featured in the It Seemed Like a Good Idea at the Time Hall of Fame.

Avalanche: Mother Nature's way of tidying the mountain.

Expedition-style climbing party: Just because you paid to climb Everest doesn't mean you belong on Everest.

Alpine style: Minimalist method, a "purer" style of dying.

Crevasse: The mountain's version of a Venus flytrap—and you're the fly.

Snow blindness: Extreme obsession that blocks out the dismal odds of survival.

Double bivy sack: A narrow bag binding you and your partner so tightly that you're forced to kill each other.

Hypoxia: High-altitude delusion that you're the next Reinhold Messner.

Snow cave: There's a fine line between *cave* and *cave-in*.

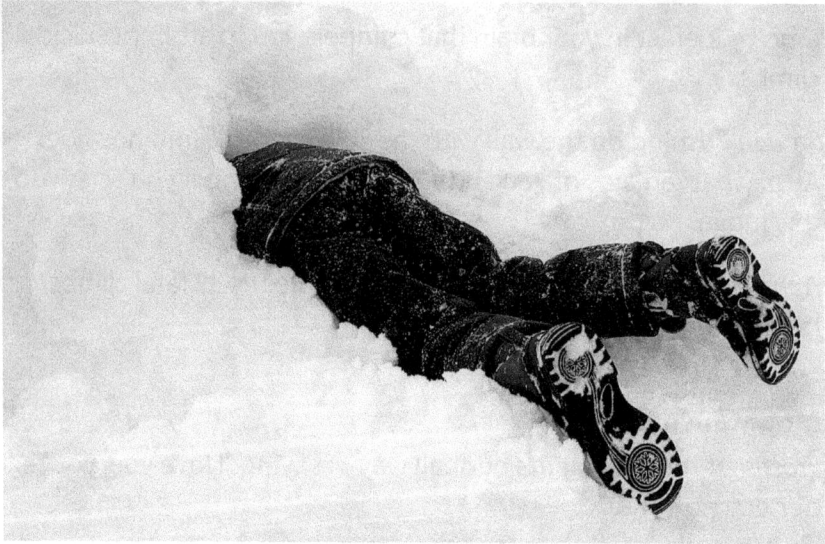

Don't light your camp stove in a snow cave.

Planning your funeral

Nobody, especially a hardass, wants to think about their own death. But this handy checklist can save you the posthumous embarrassment of looking down (or up) from your spirit's eternal abode and hearing Barry Manilow played at your memorial service.

Indicate your choices and give this list to a reliable friend—not a relative who would freak out, not a fellow hardass, and especially not anyone in your climbing party.

Tunes

"Help me, I think I'm fallin'"   Joni Mitchell

"Go ahead and jump!"   Van Halen

"I'm learning to fly, but I ain't got wings / Coming down is the hardest thing"   Tom Petty

"Free-fallin'"   Tom Petty

"I fall to pieces"   Patsy Cline

"Go rest high on that mountain"   Vince Gill   *Cliché alert: this one's been played at billions of non-climbers' funerals, but it's still a solid choice if you cash in your chips on a mountain.*

Invitation list

My hardass climber friends who are still alive:

[name #1] _____

[name #2] _____

Choose your tombstone inscription

Δ He died with his crampons on

Δ I told you that was a crevasse field

Δ Another "sewing machine leg"-related death

Δ Why would God let me fall off Thank God Ledge?

Δ Actually, I'd rather be smearing at Joshua Tree

Δ Bury my heart at Kangchenjunga

Suggestions for your eulogy

"He/she died doing what they loved…"

…gasping for breath.

…peeing off a bivy ledge.

…glomming down a dozen protein bars.

…sacrificing fingertips on El Cap.

…waiting five hours behind bumper-to-bumper climbers on Mt. Everest.

"I'm sure she/he would want us to know…"

…Life's a pitch, and then you die.

…I'm sorry I dropped out of MIT for this.

…That puja ceremony at Base Camp was a complete waste of time.

…There's a full canister of O_2 in my basement if anyone wants to use it.

…I thought the "Death Zone" was just a figure of speech.

…Shoulda crumped when I had the chance.

Rest In Permafrost

PART V
BLAB-LIOGRAPHY:
A CYNIC'S READING LIST

The Bickersons

The Mountain of My Fear and *Deborah* by David Roberts. Two Harvard undergrads bicker, wrangle and argue their way up a remote Alaskan peak, leaving both friends so emotionally battered that they do it again two years later.

Keep the home fires burning

Where the Mountain Casts Its Shadow by Maria Coffey. While climbers wait out blizzards at 20,000 feet, their spouses and kids wait & worry back home. A reminder that despite deadly cold, impenetrable terrain, blinding snowstorms and severe frostbite, extreme mountaineering has its downside.

Born to be high

The Impossible Climb: Alex Honnold, El Capitan, and the Climbing Life by Mark Synnott. Alex becomes the Neil Armstrong of extreme climbers by free-soloing Yosemite's El Capitan—but instead of a lunar lander and a space suit, he drives a beat-up van and wears ragged cutoffs. Oh, and he wasn't invited to the White House afterward, either.

Alone on the Wall by Alex Honnold with David Roberts. A study of Alex's amazing skill coupled with his remarkable modesty. Isn't he afraid of falling to his death? Alex: "It'll be the worst four seconds of my life."

"There's no need to fear—Underdog is here!"
The Push: A Climber's Search for the Path by Tommy Caldwell.
Despite being held hostage by terrorists in Kyrgyzstan, then
suffering a life-altering injury, Tommy became the best all-around
rock climber in the world. (My fellow word-nerds will appreciate
the unintentional humor of this caption: "After cutting off my left
index finger with a table saw, my doctor told me I should recon-
sider my profession as a climber.")

The world's first crawlathon
Touching the Void and *The Beckoning Silence* by Joe Simpson. A
gravely injured climber invents a new sport, the ultramarathon
crawl. Fifteen years later, after losing scores of friends and nearly
his own life (again) to the mountains, he questions when enough
is enough. Yeah, enough already!

Be very afraid
Enduring Patagonia by Gregory Crouch. A horrendous storm
traps two men at the base, each secretly glad for an excuse not
to ascend the terrifying Cerro Torre. Finally forced to climb, they
realize the ascent is a breeze compared to bivying with a guy who
hasn't showered in six years.

**Frozen: members of a climbing party
+ one climber's member**
No Way Down: Life and Death on K2 by Graham Crowley. "The killer
mountain" snuffs out 11 climbers; one of the survivors endures a
frozen penis.

Ya gotta hand it to her
Climbing Free: My Life in the Vertical World by Lynn Hill with Greg
Child. An entry in her baby journal reads: "Lynn climbs the monkey
bars like a pro." And it's all precociously uphill from there. Possibly

the only book that has ever featured a life-size photo of the author's chalky hand on its back cover.

"E.V., phone home"

No Shortcuts to the Top and *K2: Life and Death on the World's Most Dangerous Mountain* by Ed Viesturs with David Roberts. Eddie Viesturs, the All-American boy, works his way through vet school while paying his dues to become a full-time climber. On dangerous routes, knows when to hold 'em and when to fold 'em. Devoted father who always phones his wife, Paula, after descending a peak. Not a whiff of dirty laundry here. <Cynic is disappointed>

Soap opera at 24,000 ft

The Last Step: The American Ascent of K2 by Rick Ridgeway. Co-ed team members gossiping, weeping, catfighting, pulling hair—and the women are even worse.

The Everest '96 shitstorm

Part 1: Into hot air

Into Thin Air: A Personal Account of the Mt. Everest Disaster by Jon Krakauer. One amateur climber's opinion of the 1996 Everest tragedy that killed eight others. The book's criticism of climbing guide Anatoli Boukreev stirred a hornet's nest of controversy. Later, Krakauer won a Pulitzer for providing back-cover blurbs on more than 200 other books about climbing.

Part 2: So there!

The Climb: Tragic Ambitions on Everest by Anatoli Boukreev and G. Weston DeWalt. Boukreev recounts how he rescued three climbers stranded above 8,000 meters elevation. A later edition includes DeWalt's "Response to John Krakauer: *Nyaaaa nyaa nyah nyaaaa nyaa.*"

Part 3: Been there, dined that
Climbing High: A Woman's Account of Surviving the Everest Tragedy by Lene Gammelgaard, the first Scandinavian woman to summit Mount Everest. Are there *any* stakeholders who haven't weighed in by this point? Oh yes, the expedition's cooking staff, in their upcoming *Cooking on Everest 1996: Logistics of Tupperware for Leftovers*.

Dude, where's my mountain?

Annapurna: The First Conquest of an 8,000-Meter Peak by Maurice Herzog. Monsieur Herzog and a cast of thousands finally lay siege to the first 8,000-er after weeks of wandering around the Himalayas trying to find *le stupide* Annapurna in the first place. *Ehh, putain!*

Acrophobia by proxy

Above the Clouds by Anatoli Boukreev. In one outstanding color photo after another, climbers are dwarfed by astonishing Himalayan peaks covered in snow and ice, inspiring readers to decide *I'm gonna go take a long hot shower.*

A woman's place is on top

Annapurna: A Women's Place by Arlene Blum. With their cheeky slogan "A woman's place is on top," Arlene Blum's 1978 all-female team became the first Americans to climb Annapurna, the first American women's Himalayan expedition, the first American women to reach 8,000 meters (26,200 feet), and the first female expedition to summit without hearing male teammates constantly calling them "girls."

I fought the law (of gravity) and the law won

Me, Myself and I by Derek T. Shitter. The Zelig of mountain morons tells more than you ever wanted to know.

Everything Everywhere All at Once

Mountaineering: The Freedom of the Hills ed. by Eric Linxweiler and Mike Maude. Any mountaineering fact not included in this 80-pound brick isn't worth knowing—but you'll need an extra Sherpa to carry it.

THE END

ABOUT THE CRAZY AUTHOR

LEAH CARSON resides in Wisconsin, which is rather flat, and Florida, which is very flat. Both Leah and her husband Tom are leery of heights, yet they spend weeks in the Rocky Mountains every summer. Like many things in her life, that doesn't make sense.

In the photo above, she's summiting the Continental Divide—in a gondola.

Her other works include *Smartass Answers to Dumbass Questions* and a bunch of absurd 99-cent Spoofbooks like *For Pets' Sake, Arts & Crap* and *Desperately Seeking Sanity*—all available at Amazon.

www.carsonmania.com